A Glimpse Behind The Calling

The Life of a Pastor

Jeffrey A. Klick

J. Mark Fox

Scripture Translations:

Unless otherwise noted, Scripture verses are from the English Standard Version.

Acknowledgments:

Thank You Lord Jesus for Your glorious gift of salvation and thank You for allowing me to serve You in Your Kingdom! Thank you Leslie my bride for walking with me all of these years...your reward in heaven will be great. (Jeff)

I also give all glory to God for anything He has accomplished through me, and I thank Him for the best gift apart for salvation that I could ever hope for: my wife, Cindy. (Mark)

Dedications:

To my fellow pastors and co-workers in the Kingdom, I pray you will finish strong and hear from our Lord, "Well done good and faithful servant." (Jeff)

To Burke Holland, the pastor who first mentored me, and to Stephen and JL, the men who offered me a place to serve. (Mark)

Hey, That Sounds Vaguely Familiar!

Both Mark and Jeff have written multiple books. Some of the material contained in this book has been or will be used in other books and articles the authors have published. For a complete list of books by the authors, please see the author's section in the back of this book.

Contents

Introduction

Walking down the cold, sterile hallway, my thoughts were clouded. The sound of my shoes and an occasional distant beeping echoed in my ears. This was going to be rough, and no matter how many times you went through it, it never eased up. Entering the bright room, I caught sight of my young friend. She lay dying in the hospital bed. Maybe she was already dead. The machines keep her body alive, but it was hopeless. I have seen that color before. Death was here.

The doctor is talking to her bewildered husband asking him to make a decision one should never have to make — when to give up and pull the plug. The young man is in shock. One minute he seems to be aware of what is going on, the next, not so much. Is he in denial, distant, removed emotionally? Probably all of them, who would not be? As I look at his wife's gray, lifeless body, with the tubes and life support keeping it functioning, I wonder how she looks at all of this.

The husband speaks in his native language to his family on the phone. They are frantically trying to arrive before it is too late. Now he is crying again, violently sobbing into the mouthpiece in an unintelligible language to me. I do not have to understand the words; I know what he is saying. The family will not make here in time.

Later, family members weep and mascara runs. Questions abound as to, "why" and "how could a good God allow this to happen?" She has four children roughly the age of my daughter's children. What will they do? How will they respond? How can a young father possibly answer the questions that must be asked like, "Daddy, when will mommy be home?" and "Daddy, why did God let mommy die?"

Their young pastor stands in the corner with his hands in his pockets. He paces and finally sits on the couch looking ashen and overwhelmed. I know how he feels. Maybe it is his first time dealing with this, maybe not. It will not be his last if he stays in the ministry. What can he possibly say to these folks to bring comfort, or answers? Sometimes silence and tears are enough. They will have to be today since there simply are no words. If the pastor makes it long-term in the ministry, his blonde hair will probably turn gray from the pain and heartache he will walk through. Most do not make it long term. Thousands of pastors leave the ministry every year. Most quit early. My heart goes out to this young pastor as he slumps into the chair. I hurt for him and yet envy him at the same time. He is not jaded yet and perhaps he will not become so. Many become cynical and give up hope. I pray he will not.

So, why did we write this book? With the publication of seemingly endless books, why bother to write another one? Of course, the correct answer is, "The Lord told me to," and that would be true. While sitting talking to my wife one morning, I had an inspiration, or perhaps better stated, I saw a need. This has happened a time or two in my life, and on that day, the impression was strong. My first book was written after a similar event. Hearing that yet another pastor had fallen (or stepped) into immorality, my heart began to break. In a moment, the outline for a book was birthed, and *Courage to Flee* ended up being written in about two days. This book will take longer, but it is written because there is a need.

After Leslie and I finished our conversation, I went down the stairs to my office. Having learned that my memory is only as long as a pencil or keyboard in this case, I immediately began to list the chapter titles.

After working on the book for a season, setting it aside, working some more, I came to the conclusion that the book would be better written with another perspective included. After waiting, praying, and thinking, I sent a draft to a good friend of mine - J. Mark Fox. We share many similar pastoral views, yet, we are very different. Mark is an excellent writer, pastor, and brother who has followed a similar journey to mine in ministry. I know you will appreciate his insights.

While our views overlap, we have elected to write this book with our comments separated so the reader can know who said what and why. Two really are better than one, and we trust that both of our thoughts will encourage you.

The book will be primarily written from a pastor's point of view with the goal of encouraging our fellow pastors. We love pastoring, at least most of it, and by God's grace we both have been blessed to serve full time for over thirty years.

This book will also make an appeal to those who are around their pastor. Pastors are people and most are quite normal. We require sleep, recreation, friendship, loyalty, forgiveness, and a lot of grace from others. Pastors are not Jesus in the flesh, for we are often walking in our own flesh. We are not super spiritual but we need supernatural abilities to further the work of the Kingdom of Jesus. We are part of the Body of Christ and serve in a particular role. We are no better or worse than any other part of this glorious Body of believers. Every believer has a role; God has called pastors to serve as under-shepherds for the Great Shepherd.

Your role may be different, but we are all called to serve. You may not be paid to be in full time ministry, but you are a full time Christian. Because most pastors are paid to serve, this places some unique tensions in the Church. The IRS considers us dual status employees - we are considered self-employed for income tax purposes, and employees for our benefits. In the Church, we are both sheep and shepherds; part of the Body, and leaders in the Body. Called to lead by being called to serve. Often hired by a committee, but expected to lead as if that does not or should not matter. We are called to speak fearlessly to those who can remove you instantly.

There is a risk in being transparent; it makes one vulnerable. Revealed within the chapters of this book is a sneak peek into the mind, family, and inner world of a pastor. We would not pretend to speak for all pastors, but we know many would agree with what is shared. We are attempting to drop a veil that conceals a great deal of personal pain and emotional strain. Please do not use the words shared here in a way that furthers the wounds. Our enemy does not need an advocate and he certainly does not need any more assistance to destroy pastors. He is quite skilled already, and as many of us know, quite successful.

At times, our words will be directed to pastors, and in other places towards those who walk with them. While the pastors reading this may be whispering, "Amen," we pray those who support the pastors will be saying, "Yes, I want to do, or be that, for my pastor."

As we close each chapter, there will be some questions that are specifically for the pastor, and a separate set for those who support them. May you prayerfully consider these questions. These questions could also be used nicely in a small group discussion format. Please take whatever action the Lord would lead you to as you listen to that still, small voice in which He so tenderly speaks.

As you join us in this journey behind the scenes of a pastor's life, please remember your pastor in prayer. This may be the first time you have thought about your pastor through the lens we will present. Excellent! Our enemy loves to destroy pastors, and your pastor has a huge target on his back. They need prayer support and your encouragement including verbally. Have you hugged your pastor this week and told him you love and appreciate him? Have you told them that their words and actions made a difference in your life?

If you are reading this and serving as a pastor, please know that many love you, regardless of your critics. God has called you to a high task. A great reward awaits you for your faithfulness. Do not give in or give up! The pastor serves as a workhorse of the Kingdom and it is a high calling. It is also lonely, takes a toll on your family, and is often painfully misunderstood. God knows, and He loves you. So do we, and there are many others that are for you. We trust you will be encouraged as you read this book, and that the Kingdom we love will be advanced and enhanced.

Pastor Jeff Klick
Pastor J. Mark Fox

1 The Call & the Importance of Vision

Where there is no vision, the people are unrestrained. (Proverbs 29:18 NASB)

Jeff

One of my current joys is that of association with several national organizations that allow me to interact with new pastors. Often full of zeal and energy, these guys are ready to change the world for Jesus. I love passion and vision. As most of us come to realize soon enough, the passion fades and vision sometimes turns into frustration. My goal in this chapter is to help new pastors not lose either their passion or their vision, at least not completely.

Sometimes, passion and vision need to be rechanneled or tempered, but it should never be lost. If we lose the motivation of serving in the pastorate out of our God-given vision, we should quit and do something else. Of course, there are times when we want to quit, every pastor has them, but we do not because of the vision that burns in our heart.

Pastors have buzzwords and "call" or "calling" is one of them. "When did you receive the call to preach brother?" or, "How did the call to pastor unfold in your life?" we are often asked. I have heard stirring stories from people that had a strong vision, dream, personal visitation from an angel or Jesus, and then they launched themselves into ministry. God bless them. My call was not like that. In fact, I was a reluctant recruit into the pastor's life.

My Call

I never wanted to be a pastor but rather a corporate executive. I loved the fast-paced harried life of management. Endless meetings, budget pressures, staff problems, and deadlines made my adrenaline flow. How can we increase net profit while expanding facilities? Can we figure out a way to cut expenses without losing valuable personnel? How can we make the deadline that is fast approaching without blowing the overtime budget? Now that really got my blood pumping! Praying, sitting at a desk, or kneeling for hours, writing, reading and meeting with hurting people did not fit my idea of a dream job.

God, however, works in mysterious ways to accomplish His tasks. God is still using donkeys to explain His word and His will to people, even reluctant ones like me. My "call" to the ministry began while I was working my dream job description above. We moved to a small town, and joined a local church that had just built a brand new facility. Like all too many other groups, the church had a very ugly split shortly after moving into the sparkling new building. Based on some previous experiences, we chose to follow the pastor.

Since there were very few men in the church, I became his right hand man by default.

This string of events introduced me to the life of a small town church pastor. Hospital calls, leading services at the nursing home, preparing messages, and even leading citywide ecumenical services; my ministry baptism was complete. The pastor and I became good friends, and I was able to see all sides of this godly man's life. The pain, hurt, rejection, family struggles, ego, pride, love of Jesus, and just about anything else you could think of were opened to me through this relationship.

I had touched the fringe of service, pastoring and seeking the Lord for others, and the call was being formed in my life. No, Jesus did not appear to me and neither did an angel. I did not have a dream or a vision and at that point, I still did not even have an interest in pastoring. I had experienced a small taste of leading and loving others, and a tiny seed was planted.

In the midst of this introduction to pastoring, while managing thirty-two tax offices, God asked, no, better stated, God required of us to quit and move back to Kansas City. This was both heartbreaking and exciting at the same time. I knew something was up in the spirit realm, but walking away from my dream career was difficult. Death of a vision has always been hard and I saw mine slipping away.

How did I know God was calling us back to the big city? Almost every month a friend of mine who was a former employer would call me and ask me to return to work for him. My friend owned an inner city remodeling firm that specialized in government contracts. The paperwork was drowning him, so he would call me and say, "Jeff, I need you. Please come back to work for me. I will pay you whatever you want, give you full benefits and anything you need, just come back." This went on for almost three full years. Every time I would graciously refuse and hang up. The last time my buddy called, I heard that still small voice say, "You did not even pray and ask Me what I wanted." I wish I could say my response was mature and went like, "Yes, Lord, Your humble servant is listening." Mine was not.

Actually, I had to fight off being annoyed, and did not want to pray. Knowing what I did know about God, I was not about to pray! Reluctantly I shot up a shotgun prayer, "God, you really don't want me to leave here, do You?" I knew the answer. Perhaps my wife will not agree, I hoped and prayed. I was learning about listening to the counsel of my wife, and surely, she would not be willing. She, however, was definitely willing to move.

I gave my employer a 30-day notice, and about two weeks into the notice, he called me from his plush office in Denver. I could almost hear a snake whisper in his offer, but not quite.

"Jeff, how would you like to move to Colorado Springs and take over a brand new district? More money, all new offices, in fact your office has an entire wall that is glass and looks into the mountains," he seemed to hiss.

As tempting as this was, we felt that the Lord had clearly directed us to move back to KC, and it was not negotiable, not even for a zero humidity mountain view. I thanked him, endured his ridicule, and set my face like flint, Okay, it was really more like jelly, but we kept on with what we firmly believed the Lord was telling us.

Working for my friend was fun and even challenging, but we were still wondering why we were in KC enduring the humidity, instead of sitting in a new office overlooking the mountains. While we waited for direction, the Lord directed us to attend the church where both my wife and I had been introduced to Jesus. We really did not want to go back there because it had grown so large, but no other church seemed right to us. The church had experienced explosive growth and was running about 1,100 people strong. We had really enjoyed the smaller church life, but the Lord had different plans.

We began to attend, and I noticed a request for help in the weekly bulletin. The church school was looking for someone to assist with bookkeeping duties, and since I had an AA in accounting, I offered my services until they could find someone. That offer unleashed a series of events behind the scene that I could never have imagined. Phone calls, meetings, budgets, and decisions of all sorts were discussed in short order. The next Sunday the leadership of the church invited my wife and me into a conference room and made us an offer we simply could not refuse. "How would you like to make half of what you are earning now and work harder than you can even imagine?" Well, one really does not get an offer like that every day, so we accepted.

I was hired as the first administrator of a church that I really did not want to attend. Welcome to the ministry! Over the next eleven years, the church grew from 1,100 to over 3,500 members. Thus began a lifetime of experience in a twenty-five year old Associates of Arts educated guy. The fast-paced meetings, pressure deadlines, budget issues, and almost everything I gave up in the corporate world, was present in this church and school. I was a new man!

The point of this story is that each one of us has a different call to the ministry, but we all have one if we are in the pastorate. Yours may be different from mine, but you are there by God's calling and choice. Perhaps you dreamed of it from the day you were old enough to understand, or maybe like me, you were drafted and somewhat reluctant. We are called to a high calling, and we serve in this capacity because God has placed us there. Once we are there, and we are sure we are supposed to be there, the vision should kick in.

Vision

Gene[1] (not his real name) called me and wanted to get together for lunch. "I want to pick your brain," he said. Little does Gene know that there really is not much to find there, but I will go along with him for the fellowship and the meal. Most pastors love to talk and eat. Perhaps that is why so many pastors struggle with weight issues, but I will leave that rabbit trail unexplored.

Gene had heard the "call" to pastor a church. Excitement was in his voice and dreams flowed from his mouth between bites. Phrases like: "I want to change the city for Jesus," and "I can't wait to start preaching!" bubbled out.

When a young pastor contacts me (like Gene), and wants to discuss the ins and outs of ministry, I always begin with their vision. I ask open-ended questions like:

- What drives you?
- What do you want to impart to those that God adds to you?
- If you could open up people's minds and place something inside of them what would it be?
- Where are you going and can you explain it?
- What burns in your heart and spirit that you can't wait to share with others?

These questions should at least be considered before attempting to lead others. We do not have to know everything but we should at least know what our passion and vision is. Gene did not. Gene just wanted to preach. While commendable, Gene will probably not make it long term as a

---

[1] This section on vision can also be found in *Pastoral Helmsmanship: A Pastor's Guide to Church Administration* - published 2014

pastor without a vision. If people do follow Gene, they will most likely become frustrated because he does not know where he is going.

Vision is freeing and confining at the same time. Vision defines where we are heading. Like railroad tracks, vision allows us to move along smoothly. Trains do not move well without tracks - and neither do pastors without a vision. The train speeds along on smooth tracks. Yet, when derailed it stops, often crashing while causing great noise and damage. A pastor without vision is akin to a train off the tracks.

What is your passion? What is burning in your soul? What comes out when you share with others? What is going to define you, and help you evaluate how you are succeeding in doing it? Vision.

> *"Without a vision the people perish or run unrestrained," states Proverbs.*

> *"With a vision people are saved and run in a proper direction," states Jeff.*

Vision defines us. Vision guides and directs our efforts. Vision brings clarity to the cloud of confusion, and helps cut through the plethora of opportunities chasing too few minutes. Vision is foundational and critical. So what is yours?

My vision is different from yours, and yours will be uniquely your own. God did not create duplicate people. If God has called you, then He has placed within you a vision that only you can fulfill. What drives your thoughts and burns within your heart? What always ends up coming out in your messages regardless of the text preached? No matter the verse or book, eventually you end up there. Mine deals with the restoration of the family and the practical aspects of how it is worked out in our daily walk with Jesus. Yours could be evangelism, discipleship, youth, missions, the lonely, helpless, poor, rich, singles, history, or any number of issues. Each of us is different. We are all unique expressions of Christ, and we will reflect His calling differently.

For me, vision brings clarity and freedom. In one respect, a church is not different from a household, we both receive a multitude of solicitations. I receive calls, emails, and yes, even snail mail every week from those that "feel led" to minister to my church family. In addition, many would invite us to join them in their service to the planet...at least enjoy our money helping them. While the validity of these requests is not necessarily the issue, the fitting into our vision clearly is.

Our church has a specific vision that we believe God has led us to follow. The freedom to refuse to participate in everyone else's vision is gained because of the vision we possess. If someone asks us to invite him or her into our service, it is a simple matter to see if his or her vision aligns with ours. If not, then the answer is no. If yes, then the answer is maybe. After prayer and discussion, we will consider the event or giving opportunity and our participation. It may be something we do, it may not be, but having a clear vision makes these decisions much easier.

Having a strong, clear vision does not mean you never step outside of it and partner with someone or give to someone else's ministry, but it does mean that the bulk of your decisions if you should is much clearer and easier to make.

If we want people to follow us, we must have some general idea of where we are heading. We must have an idea of how to get there and how to make corrections when we swerve off the plan. As I mentioned, our vision is primarily focused on the restoration of the family to health. Our desire as a church body is to learn how Christianity is supposed to be lived out day by day in a very practical manner, beginning in our homes. Our vision is clear and measurable.

This vision is expounded in eleven points called cleverly enough, "Our Vision Statement." While we are not doing everything in our statement every day, this is one of our founding documents, and it includes guiding principles that we attempt to follow. For example, one of our goals is to help marriages. We desire to see a reduction in the divorce rate among believers and to see a husband and wife grow together in oneness in Christ. Therefore, I will often teach a message that has some points centered on how a particular Scripture actually makes a difference in a godly marriage. I will not teach a marriage seminar every week, but every week the vision is reinforced somehow or someway.

Everything we end up doing at our church will be filtered through the vision. If something is contrary to the vision, we will not do it. If something enhances our calling and vision, we most likely will do it. The issue is not a matter of whether the potential activity or ministry has a valid purpose. The issue is, does it enhance or reinforce our vision?

In practice then, every sermon, activity, printed document, event, and whatever else takes place in our church body should tie back somehow to the vision, or we should question if the action fits into what God has called us to accomplish. Vision is freeing.

If you are a pastor who is reading this, what does it all mean to you? What if you were hired into a church or onto a staff that already has a strong vision in place and perhaps their vision is not yours? This does not mean that your vision has to die. Maybe your vision can be repackaged or slowly adopted over time. Of course, it is easier to start a church than to take over one, but the vision is still critical either way.

When I was hired at the large church, my vision was still being formed. I was clearly the low man on the organizational chart. As I served and gained experience, my right to share and speak grew. Eventually I was added to the elder board and I served on the Executive Committee that made all of the day-to-day decisions. This greatly enhanced my ability to share the vision God had given me. The vision deepened, and the leadership warmed to many of my ideas and concepts. As the years rolled by it became time for me to move on and start my own church. This opportunity came in a package that I did not want or expect but God was still ruling and directing.

Through a series of painful events in 1993, I resigned my position at this large church and sought the Lord regarding what I should do next. It became apparent that we were to begin a brand new work with a fresh vision, and we did so two months later. God works in interesting ways, and this book is an example of His efforts.

I have learned that painful conclusions of one season often give birth to delightful introductions into the next one. While I still don't relish the process, change, (and sometimes painful change) should be embraced and often yields wonderful fruit.

Is the Vision Unchangeable?

Another issue many pastors face is trying to change or modify their vision in an established church. One day I had lunch with a pastor serving in a denominational church. The pastor was really struggling with where he was in the implementation of his vision. The pastor had a heart to make a significant change in the direction of his church, but he just did not see how it was possible. The pastor uttered a sentence that I have not been able to forget:

"Our church is so much in debt that if we make a change, and we lose one family, we will go under."

My heart broke for the man, but I did understand his dilemma. Churches sometimes are trapped in debt. Pastors become fearful of offending those who pay their salary or are large givers. Money is important, and while we are not to love it, we sure have a hard time living without it. So do churches. This is a sad reality that many pastors face — the tension between preaching and teaching the truth—- verses running the risk of offending those that pay the bills.

If we are to be pastors of integrity, then we must teach the truth in love. Ultimately, God is our source of provision, and we cannot allow any other to take His place. That does not mean, however, that we should not use wisdom and prudence in our efforts to implement the vision we embrace. We need to be aware of the financial pressure and walk carefully when we share hard truth.

If we need to make changes to the church's vision, we should proceed prayerfully and carefully. We must invest the time to win the hearts, minds, and confidence of those we lead. Our leadership team, boards, and key people must be won over to our point of view. If we are really hearing from the Lord with the change we have in mind, He can change people's points of view.

Here is a truth that I have learned that might help:

The decision reached is often not as important as the processed used to reach it.

Maintaining our key relationships is important. A divided church will not stand and it is far better to slow down on change than to ram it down someone's throat that is not ready for it. God is not in a hurry, and we should not be either. If what we think we need to change is from God, then we will have the wisdom and grace to help bring others along. If we only face resistance on every front, perhaps we need to lay it down and wait. It is much more palatable for those who follow us to make five-degree rather than ninety-degree ones.

Mark

My Call

It was 1972 and I was sitting with my family in church on a Sunday night. There was an evangelist speaking that evening, and I could not begin to tell you what his name was. I can't see his face in my memory, either. But I will never forget the way the Lord used him to speak to me that evening, not long after my fifteenth birthday.

At some point in his message, the evangelist said the Lord was looking for young people who would answer the call to the ministry. I squirmed in my seat because I believed that the man was looking at me and speaking directly to me when he said it. At the same time, I felt a stirring in my spirit. I had only been a Christian for a few months, having met Jesus on the mountaintop during a youth retreat that summer at Ridgecrest Baptist Assembly. But I had been a church-goer my whole life, and I was very familiar with the Baptist preacher's passion for asking for people to commit their lives to the Lord in their seat, and then come down front and make it public. I knew when the evangelist said that night that he wanted the young people who believed they were being called into the ministry to come down front, I had to go. I was propelled out of my seat, bringing shock to my father and a blush of pride to my mother. I walked down the aisle, past my friends who also looked on with surprise, and met the preacher in front of the communion table. It was that night that I told the Lord I would be a minister of the Gospel. I had no idea what that meant. I just knew that I loved the One who saved my soul, and I wanted to serve Him with my life and, if He would have me, with my vocation.

This happened at the same time that a handful of us had come down from the mountaintop with changed hearts. I came back from Ridgecrest with a new understanding that Jesus Christ is the Son, and my life revolves around Him. I went back to the youth meetings at our church with a new spirit...literally. I told the youth pastor that what had happened to some of us at Ridgecrest was too good to keep to ourselves. "We need to tell everybody we know," I said.
I didn't know about the four lepers starving to death outside the Samarian gate in 2 Kings 7, but we were in the same situation. Those guys were going to die. The city was under siege by the Syrians, who were camped outside the city and slowly starving the Samarians to death. The four lepers looked at each other one day and said, "Why are we sitting here? If we sit here, we die. If we go into the city, we die. Why don't we go surrender to the Syrians? What is the worst thing that could happen to us? Oh, yeah, we could die. But, we might not!" So, they traipsed off to the Syrian's encampment. Meanwhile, God had caused the Syrian soldiers to hear something that wasn't there, the presence of chariots and a huge army, and they had all fled from camp, leaving everything they owned behind. The four lepers stumbled into the deserted camp bug-eyed, not believing their good fortune, going from tent to tent eating, gathering silver and gold, eating some more, scavenging, eating, until they suddenly stopped, gravy dripping off their chins. They said, "We are not doing right. This day is a day of good news,

and we remain silent. If we wait until morning light, some punishment will come upon us. Now therefore, let us go and tell the king's household." (2 Kings 7:3-9)

That's the way I felt after my conversion: though I deserved death, I had stumbled onto life that I had never dreamed even existed. I know now that God did it all, just as He did for those four lepers. He led me to Ridgecrest, He apprehended me there by grace through faith, and He brought me down to the valley with a vision for reaching others. I could not keep this to myself. Oh, no. "Evangelism is like one beggar telling another beggar where he found some bread." Except I didn't find it. God found me. And it wasn't just bread; it was the Bread of everlasting Life. And I was not a beggar; I wasn't even interested in the things of God when He met me on the mountaintop and won my heart.

Five of us met with the youth pastor, and we told him that we wanted to start inviting our friends to come to the youth meeting on Monday night, but there was a twist. First, we said, we want to actually go to their houses and sing some songs and give them our testimony. He was a bit skeptical of how well this was going to work, but he said to go for it and sent us off with his blessing. That next day was a Monday, so we started talking to our friends about what had happened to us at Ridgecrest. And we lined up our first prospect for Monday night visitation. We showed up at his doorstep at around 6:30 or so, five of us with two guitars. He nervously invited us into his living room, and we plopped down on the chairs and sofas and began our planned presentation. It was very simple. "Bob," we would say, "We went to summer camp last week at Ridgecrest in the mountains, and something very exciting happened there."

"Really? Uh, what was that?"

"Bob," we would say, "we met Jesus."

Then we would sing a few songs we had learned at camp. One was written by Larry Norman, and it was called, *Sweet, Sweet Song of Salvation*. It was a catchy little tune and included some clapping and some "nah, nahs," and the chorus went as follows:

> Sing that sweet, sweet song of salvation
> And let your laughter fill the air
> Sing that sweet, sweet song of salvation
> Tell all the people everywhere.
> Sing that sweet song of salvation
> To every land and every nation
> Sing that sweet, sweet song of salvation
> And let the people know that Jesus cares.

We would get into that song, sing it at the top of our lungs. And we loved the words of the first verse:

> When you know a pretty story
> You don't let it go unsaid
> You tell it to your children
> Before you tuck 'em into bed.
> And if you know a wonderful secret
> Well, you gotta' tell it to all of your friends
> You tell 'em that a lifetime filled with Jesus
> Is like a street that never ends.

"Bob, we know a wonderful secret, and we just had to come and tell it to one of our friends." One of us would share our testimony of how Jesus Christ had saved us, and how our lives were changed because of His sacrifice for us on the cross. Then we would sing another song, possibly an old

James Taylor favorite:

> When you're down and troubled
> And you need a helping hand
> And nothing, whoa nothing is going right.
> Close your eyes and think of me
> And soon I will be there
> To brighten up even your darkest nights.
> You just call out my name,
> And you know wherever I am
> I'll come running, running, yeah
> To see you again.
> Winter, spring, summer, or fall,
> All you have to do is call
> And I'll be there, yeah, yeah, yeah.
> You've got a friend.

We would sing it loud and soulfully, just like James did, only not quite so nasally, and then we would end our visit with, "Bob, there's no friend like Jesus. All of your other friends, ourselves included, will come running to help you when we can, but we can only come some of the time, and we can only help with some of your problems. Only Jesus can come and help anytime. Only Jesus can solve all of your problems. Only Jesus can save you from your sins. Would you be interested in learning more about Jesus with us? Because we are going back to the church now to meet with the youth pastor and study the Bible together, and we would love for you to come with us."

More often than not, "Bob" answered yes. And for the record, we only went to Bob's house once. By the next summer, that group of five teenagers had grown to more than fifty. Revival was taking place at our church, and not just with the youth. Many of the teens who started coming to church and were born again began to invite their parents and their siblings to come. Some of the parents had faithfully dropped their teens off at church for months before they started coming on Sunday themselves. I remember that one of the young men we had invited to church in those days, named Mike, became a Christian. He started in on his father to become one, too, and his father saw the transformation that only Christ can do as He worked in his son. It wasn't long before Mike's father was led to Christ by the pastor, Burke Holland.

As you can see, my calling coincided with a powerful opportunity the Lord gave me to be a witness to my friends, and to see many of them and their families come to Christ. I was convinced by now that the Lord wanted me to serve Him in full-time ministry, but I was also torn with a desire to do other things as well, particularly in acting. I loved the stage and I could see myself making that a career one day as well. So I spoke to my pastor about that, and he said something I will never forget and I have repeated to many young men who have told me they are considering the ministry as a vocation. Pastor Holland said, "Mark, if you can do anything else besides ministry, do it." I didn't understand, and told him so. "I can do a lot of things, Pastor Holland," I replied. "I think I could make it as an actor." "Then do that instead," he said. "Because ministry is a calling, and only those who know they cannot live if they have to do anything else should enter into it. You will not survive what you will have to go through in ministry if it is not a calling from God."

I took several left turns over the next few years in college, and even headed into a master's degree in Oral Interpretation of Literature, thinking I would pursue acting as a career or get a PhD and teach in college. God brought Cindy into my life as I finished my master's, and used her walk with Jesus to turn me back to Him and to my calling. I started a youth ministry in 1982, traveled with an evangelistic music team from 1984 to 1986, and then started Antioch Community Church with four other families in 1987. I became the pastor the next year, and have been there ever since.

In the next chapter, we want to explore the workload of a pastor, and how we are supposed to be spending our time. Most of us are asked at least once in our life, "What do you do anyway, since you only work one hour a week?" The question reflects a bit of humor and a perhaps an unintended insult.

Reflection Points for Pastors:

1. Do I know that God has called me into the ministry? If so, how do I know?

2. What is burning deep down in my spirit that I long to share with others?

3. Have I given thanks to the Lord recently for allowing me to walk with Him and share His great plans for others?

4. If I could share just one truth with people, what would it be?

Reflection Points: Those Who Support Them:

1. Do I know my pastor's vision and can I explain it?
2. Do I share and support it, if not all of it, how much?
3. Do I know my pastor's story or his calling? Will I make time to find it out from him?
4. Is my pastor struggling with discouragement? How would I know?

Called to Study and Pray

What do you do with all your time since you only work one hour a week?

Jeff

After leaving the large church and starting a new work, I went through a period of adjustment. That really is an understatement for the first six months of my new pastorate felt like a long, slow walk through the fog. I was used to sixteen scheduled meetings a week and dozens more that just seemed to happen arising from constant pressing problems. A fast paced, quickly changing, and heavily staff centered office life had found a deep place in me. From 7:30am to 5:00pm most days and several nights a week, I was busy.

Now what? Each day I would get up, walk downstairs to my office, and wonder to myself, "What was I supposed to be doing anyway?"

The life of the solo pastor of a small church is very different from that of one with a large staff. Where would I find fellowship? Who would help with all the detail stuff that I was not very good at accomplishing? I was used to action and distraction but now I had quiet, and lots of it. What is it that pastors are supposed to be doing anyway? An excellent question to consider.

One important aspect of our life is of course our teaching ministry. Most pastors are called upon to teach at least once a week and for many, multiple times. The only way to appreciate what goes into preparing a sermon is to prepare one. In my church, we invite brothers to share on Wednesday nights. The brothers are required to put together a thirty-minute message that makes sense and has a point to it. This can be more challenging than they think. After giving a message, the brother will typically have one of two responses. They will either say they could not believe how hard it was to come up with thirty minutes of material, or how hard it was to get it down to a half hour. The man can now relate to one major aspect of preparing messages or sermons. It takes a great deal of time to study, edit, practice, and think through just one message. Imagine if your pastor presents two or more per week.

Many people expect their pastor to hit a home run every time they are up at bat. While it would be nice to do so, reality just does not work out that way. It is one thing to have a month to prepare for a Wednesday message and quite another to have only a few days. Not only do you have to put the message together but also it has to be well illustrated, relevant, inspiring, and must appeal to all listeners at all times. No pressure, just be perfect. In addition, do not just be perfect once, but every time. Fifty-two times a year. Or, one hundred four. Or, one hundred fifty-six...

The point is not to complain, for every pastor I know loves to preach and teach. What most people do not understand is the pressure. We want to teach the Word of God in such a way as to bring glory to God and help to those that are listening, *every time* we speak. If we are to have something of value to pass on to those following us we must allow time for study, prayer, and quiet. While we may only speak one hour a week, most studies reveal that pastors work in excess of sixty hours a week.

Part of my adjustment to a smaller church from the large one, or even the corporate world, was how to count my work hours. Going to an office every day was easy compared to walking downstairs to the basement. How many hours is enough each day? What part of my day should be devoted to prayer and seeking God and how do I know when I have prayed enough? How many hours a day should be devoted to reading the Word of God, studying current events to stay relevant and informed, reading the classics to bring depth, theology to assure accuracy, and what about personal development? How much time should be given to continuing education, technology, social networks, and relationship building? Being unsupervised and without an established schedule was difficult for me at first.

What about social calls and how to accurately count them during the workday? If you are invited over for dinner to become acquainted are you on the clock, or is this personal? If we wander into marriage counseling or child raising tips, have we moved into a work situation or are we still just socializing? When is the pastor not on call? Keeping track of hours worked gets confusing. Are we just being friends or am I serving as a pastor right now? Throw in ministry opportunities, small groups, prayer and leadership meetings, hospital visits and phone calls, and a week can fill up quickly.

A pastor's schedule can be hard to explain to those who are not pastors, but includes praying, studying, preparing, serving, building relationships, and meetings. It is sometimes difficult to discern what is personal and what is ministry in all of a pastor's relationships. Every job and profession has its challenges and being a pastor is no different.

Someone sooner or later will ask the famous, supposed to be a funny question to their pastor:

> *"What do you do all week, since you only work for one hour?"*

Please refrain from saying that to your pastor for it is not funny and it is not true, and in fact, it is really a slap in the face. Most pastors work hard, often endure major criticism, and are typically not paid what they are worth. Most of the pastors I know love the Lord, love their people, and even love the insensitive person that asks such a foolish question. Most pastors are selfless people that are willing to lay down their lives for the sheep under their care at just about any hour day or night. Please do not criticize them until you have walked in their wingtips for a bit.

Here are some other unintended, even humorous slaps that pastors hear:

- "Hey pastor, the message today was really good. What did you do differently?"
- "Wow pastor, your message today was on target. Most of the time they don't apply to me, but today's sure did."

- "Something has changed, you were really animated today."
- "Must not have had much to do this week, your message was very deep today."

Ouch. Backhanded compliments often leave a scar and even amps up the feeling of pressure to perform. We have all said things we wish we wouldn't have, but thinking before speaking will encourage your pastor. Humor that is insulting hurts and though the pastor may laugh, he may also walk away wondering how much of what was said was true.

Equip the Saints

So, what are we supposed to be doing, pastors? Excellent question. While it will vary, depending on the size of the church and the particular role each pastor is assigned, there are some common elements from a biblical perspective. There are senior pastors, executive ministers, youth, music, elderly, children's, singles, and family pastors. There are solo pastors, and some that are part of a huge staff. There are administratively gifted pastors and others that are great speakers. Some are relational and some are loners, but all of us have some basic responsibilities according to the Scriptures.

> *And he gave the apostles, the prophets, the evangelists, the shepherds and teachers, to equip the saints for the work of ministry, for building up the body of Christ, until we all attain to the unity of the faith and of the knowledge of the Son of God, to mature manhood, to the measure of the stature of the fullness of Christ... (Ephesians 4:11-13)*

If we are called to be a shepherd, we are called to equip the saints to do the work of the ministry. We are supposed to be about helping to build up the Body of Christ and we are to help people mature. The word "equip" has at its root the idea of fixing what is broken, or to restore back to a normal, healthy state of operation. Regardless of where we may serve in the Body of Christ, we must be about the work of helping to restore what is broken. Just about any pastor will eventually end up dealing with brokenness. Almost every pastor will deal with broken families, marriages, interpersonal relationships, those scarred by sin, the lost, poor, and the sick. All of these situations deal with fixing what needs repaired. Pastors need to equip in this sense of the word - to help restore what is broken.

> *So I exhort the elders among you, as a fellow elder and a witness of the sufferings of Christ, as well as a partaker in the glory that is going to be revealed; shepherd the flock of God that is among you, exercising oversight, not under compulsion, but willingly, as God would have you; not for shameful gain, but eagerly; not domineering over those in your charge, but being examples to the flock.*
> *(1 Peter 5:1-3)*

Peter is clear as to one aspect of our lives as pastors — be an example to the flock. In addition, while we are being that example, please keep checking the motives. Are we serving because we love to or because we have to? Are we serving for a paycheck or an eternal reward? Are we serving or domineering? We need to make sure we are doing what is right and for the correct reasons.

If our sheep could follow us around every day, what would they see? What are we doing and how are we doing it? Would we have to change anything we do or say if our people were with us? People are always watching us; what do they see? No matter the descriptive title in front of "pastor" — youth, singles, senior or associate — we all have people watching and listening to us.

There are no perfect pastors, only a perfect Savior, but we must be aware of what we are commanded — "be an example" is clear, even in the Greek. We are commanded to show people how to live the Christian life by how we live ours. Ouch.

Since we are not perfect, part of what people will see is how to repent, ask for forgiveness, and our willingness to get back up after a fall. We all stumble and we all fail, but Jesus bids us to keep on walking with Him. We will show to others what we really believe by how we act. We will be given multiple opportunities to forgive others, to overlook offenses, to esteem others as better than ourselves, and to take up our cross daily. In other words, we will demonstrate how to live the Christian life.

Peter did not stop there however:

> *And when the chief Shepherd appears, you will receive the unfading crown of glory. (1 Peter 5:4)*

There is an unfading crown of glory for the under-shepherds who do not quit. We do not know how all that works in heaven but I can picture my Lord and Savior walking up to me and saying, "Well done good and faithful shepherd, here is your crown that will never fade." Glory is an excellent word! We are called to help, to endure, and to help fix what is broken in others, just as Jesus did. What a glorious calling and what an awesome reward that awaits those who do not quit!

As pastors, we are called to a life of prayer, meditation, reflection, and study. Many of us are called upon to share what we learn and hear from these times alone with our Shepherd. Whether we share to thousands or to just one person we are there to help fix what is broken and to lay down our lives for the sheep. We are walking in the footsteps of our Shepherd, and pursuing Jesus is a high calling that we must take seriously.

My friend Lyn asked me about the private prayer life of pastors. Pastors that she had interacted with were often so busy that they did not have time to develop their own personal walk with God. This is a constant battle for pastors. Many pastors are called upon to counsel, teach, lead groups and each of these can take an emotional toll. By constantly pouring out your life for others, there is a drain spiritually and emotionally. Pastors must recharge and refill in order to make sure they have a reservoir.

If we hope to make it long term in the ministry, we had better allow some time for personal renewal. We scour the Scriptures looking for sermon ideas, but sometimes we need to just soak in the Word of God for our own benefit. We pray for others, but we also need time to meditate and wait upon the Lord to renew our own strength. If we ignore our own renewal times, we will soon have little to share with others. We must make time to wait.

> *Even youths shall faint and be weary, and young men shall fall exhausted; but they who wait for the LORD shall renew their strength; they shall mount up with wings like eagles; they shall run and not be weary; they shall walk and not faint.*
> *(Isaiah 40:30-31)*

Mark

I believe in pastors for the local church. I am one. And I believe in the primacy of preaching in the local church. There's a good reason why the Apostles asked the church in Jerusalem to find seven men who could serve tables in Jerusalem when there was problem with the Greek widows being overlooked. They said,

> *"It is not right that we should give up preaching the word of God to serve tables…we will devote ourselves to prayer and to the ministry of the Word."*
> *(Acts 6:2-4)*

I had to learn how to preach the old-fashioned way. I learned what good preaching is by doing a lot of bad preaching. But I discovered along the way that God has indeed called me to preach, and the gift grows with use. In his book, *If You Want to Walk on Water, You Have to Get Out of the Boat,* John Ortberg tells a story he found in another book entitled, *Art and Fear.*

> "A ceramics teacher divided his class into two groups. One group would be graded solely on quantity of work—fifty pounds of pottery would be an 'A,' forty would be a 'B,' and so on. The other group would be graded on quality. Students in that group had to produce only one pot—but it had better be good. **Amazingly, the highest quality pots were turned out by the quantity group.**[2]" (emphasis mine)

[2] John Ortberg, *If You Want to Walk on Water, You Have to Get Out of the Boat,* (Zondervan, 2008). p. 209

It seems that while the quantity group kept churning out pots, they were continually learning from their disasters and growing as artists. The quality group sat around theorizing about perfection and worrying about it—but they never actually got any better." And *that's* why my wife and I have seven kids! We just keep trying to get it right...! Just kidding. But there *is* a powerful principle at work here for preachers. You learn to preach by preaching.

That is why I agree with Jeff and believe we pastors need to give other men of God an opportunity to hone the gift of preaching as well. If we are "convulsively clinging to the pulpit," that opportunity will not be there. Having said that, we *are* called to protect the flock, and shepherd them with care. That means that we *do* guard the pulpit. If a man in the church tells me he thinks he is called to preach, I do not immediately schedule him for a Sunday morning sermon. He may be like the man who was convinced he was called to preach but every time he did so, the people would either be squirming in their seats, or falling asleep, or looking for any excuse they could find to slip out of the pew and go out to the foyer or the bathroom or check the stove at home! When this was gently pointed out to the man who thought he was called to preach, he replied, "Well, I am sure I have been called to preach; I guess these folks just aren't called to listen!" The truth is, if someone is truly called to preach, he will have listeners, and what he teaches will bear fruit. So, if Brother Joe wants to get up in the pulpit and preach, I will first give him some smaller tests. I will ask him to share at our home group. There is a much smaller crowd there, maybe 20-35 people, and much less potential for damage to the hearers *or* the speaker! If that goes well, I may ask him to speak at a Men's Breakfast. There are maybe 45-55 men and young men at those, but the atmosphere is casual and the men know that any one of their brothers may be standing up to address them; they do not come expecting a polished presentation. I may ask him to share his testimony in one of our meetings. The point is, the elders and I guard the pulpit by not allowing just anybody to have the 40-55 minute preaching slot.

Let me address three important questions pastors should answer about preaching.

First, why do we preach? Simply stated, preaching is central to the health of the church. The Word of God is center stage, and must be given time in every gathering of God's people on Sunday morning or in the mid-week service. Paul said it "pleased God through the foolishness of the message preached to save those who believe." (1 Corinthains 1:21) In his excellent book, "*The Priority of Preaching*," Christopher Ash builds a case for preaching from the Word of God. "The authority of God was mediated to Israel not by the written word but by the written word *preached*.[3]" And quoting Calvin, "The reason a man climbs into the pulpit is, 'that God may speak to us by the mouth of a man.[4]'"

And to those who want to just watch a DVD of preaching or even a satellite feed, Ash writes, "As William Sangster put it, there can be no substitute 'for a Spirit-filled man looking men in the face and speaking the Word of God to their consciences and hearts.[5]" To the world, there is nothing sillier than for a man to stand behind a lectern with an ancient book and babble about it for 45 minutes to an hour every Sunday morning. Al Mohler said,

> "If you want to see quick results, the preaching of the Word just might not be the way to go. If you are going to find results in terms of statistics, numbers, and

[3] Christopher Ash, *The Priority of Preaching,* (Christian Focus Publications, 2009), p. 26
[4] Ibid, p. 43
[5] Ibid, p. 43

> visible response, it just might be that there are other mechanisms, other programs, and other means that will produce that faster. The question is whether it produces Christians.[6]"

The Gospel is the power of God to those who believe!

The pulpit is to be honored in the church and the man of God who breaks open the bread on Sunday morning must approach that task with the greatest of reverence and fear. As Paul said, "I was with you in weakness, in fear, and in much trembling." (1 Corithians 2:3) Why do we tremble at the task that has been put before us? Because as Alistair Begg has said so well, "When the Word of God is truly preached, the voice of God is clearly heard." Who is sufficient for such things? Only by God's grace can any of us stand in the pulpit and preach. But by God's grace we must do that. Do not let anything take the place of the pulpit in your church, brothers. Don't let anything take the place of your time in study and in prayer.

Second, what do we preach? I believe one of the greatest benefits to the church that I pastor happened about 11 years ago when I finally made a commitment to expository preaching. I can look back over the years at my sermon book, where I have recorded all the sermon titles and texts I have preached at least as far back as 1990, and there were many times when I would do an extended series on the Sermon on the Mount, or the Ten Commandments, or a section in Romans. But then I would go back to topical preaching and do a long series on discipleship or spiritual warfare or the church. But then I finally heard it from the Lord and understood it clearly: the church I pastor will be best fed as I and others take them through whole books of the Bible, verse

[6] http://www.brenthobbs.com/preachingquotes.html

by verse. Like Isaiah said, "line upon line, line upon line, here a little, there a little." (Isaish 28:13) Paul said to the Ephesian elders, "For I did not shrink from declaring to you the whole counsel of God." (Acts 20:27) I have an idea that the three years he spent teaching the church in Ephesus was spent going through the books of the Old Testament.

When Jesus met the two fellows on the road to Emmaus after Jesus' resurrection, He took them through Moses and the prophets, expounding to them "in all the Scriptures the things concerning Himself." (Luke 24:27) Expository preaching, then, at its very foundation, is a commitment to the sufficiency of Scripture. Ligon Duncan defined it as,

> "...the faithful explanation and application of the Bible in which the text of Scripture supplies the manner of the preacher's exhortations rather than the preacher using the text as an occasion for his own expostulations, however helpful they may be.[7]"

Finally, how do we preach? We preach with clarity and with conviction, with power and with precision, with great delight in the Word of God as **truth** and as a two-edged sword that is able to cut right down into the hearts of men and women and bring life change! Boring preaching should be outlawed from all our churches. Again, Alistair Begg said, "The reason most preaching is ignored today is that it deserves to be."

There is a tale told of the great English actor William Macready. An eminent preacher once said to him: "I wish you would explain to me something." Macready answered, "Well, what is it? I don't know that I can explain anything to a preacher." The preacher said, "What is the reason for the

---

[7] http://www.brenthobbs.com/preachingquotes.html

difference between you and me? You are appearing before crowds night after night with fiction, and the crowds come wherever you go. I am preaching the essential and unchangeable truth, and I am not getting any crowd at all." Macready's answer was this: "This is quite simple. I can tell you the difference between us. I present my fiction as though it were truth; you present your truth as though it were fiction." John Piper said,

> "Lack of intensity in preaching can only communicate that the preacher has never been seriously gripped by the reality of which he speaks - or that the subject matter is insignificant.[8]"

May God help us preach His Word faithfully.

Before we move into looking at what else we do as pastors, let's stop for a moment and reflect quietly before our Lord and see if He wants to add anything here.

Reflection Points for Pastors:

1. Do I spend enough time being quiet in my week? Can I do anything about that answer?

2. Have I communicated to others what I do with my time? Am I accountable to someone?

3. Have I forgiven those that have hurt me with insensitive comments?

4. Do I need to refocus any part of my ministry after reading this chapter?

---

[8] http://www.brenthobbs.com/preachingquotes.html

Reflection Points: Those Who Support Them:

1. Have I misjudged my pastor and how they spend their time?
2. Do I have unrealistic expectations for my pastor?
3. Have I prayed for them recently to have peace, joy, and rest?
4. Have I held my pastor to a different standard than I hold myself?

3 Called to Serve

The greatest among you shall be your servant.
Matthew 23:11

Jeff

The disciples of Jesus must have experienced some amazing events — demons screaming, storms ceasing, bread and fish multiplying, and the dead walking and talking. We know that the disciples themselves participated in miracles with healings and even demons being cast out, for Luke tells us so in chapter 10. Pretty ego-building stuff for a rag tag bunch of poor guys.

The very Word of God was explaining the truth of God to them and I am sure they marveled. For three years, the group traveled around while discussing God's Kingdom with the King Himself. Several times, we are given insight into the discussions the disciples had while Jesus was busy doing something else. For example:

> *And they came to Capernaum. And when he was in the house he asked them, "What were you discussing on the way?" But they kept silent, for on the way they had argued with one another about who was the greatest. And he sat down and called the twelve. And he said to them, "If anyone would be first, he must be last of all and servant of all." And he took a child and put him in the midst of them, and taking him in his arms, he said to them, "Whoever receives one such child in my name receives me, and whoever receives me, receives not me but him who sent me."*
> *(Mark 9:33-37)*

Jesus knew that they had been discussing (correction, ARGUING) about which one of *them* was the greatest. Interesting. They were with the Master, the Creator, the I AM, the Living Word, Great Shepherd, Lord of Lords and King of Kings, yet they were fighting about which of *them* was the greatest. For all they had learned at Jesus' feet they had not quite understood this lesson yet. The way up in Jesus' kingdom is down, or perhaps better stated, through service.

Pastors are called to serve, not to be served. We should have the righteous desire to lead: in service, in self-sacrifice, death-to-self choices, and the laying down of our will for the sake of others. We are supposed to set an example for the flock to follow and we should follow our Shepherd's example of service. Jesus was the highest, yet became the lowest. He was God, yet emptied Himself for us. He who knew no sin became sin for us, and it cannot possibly get any lower than that!

Servant leadership is a term that has been around for a long while, yet what does it mean where you and I live? What does it look like in our homes and churches? How about in our leadership meetings and small groups? There is a tension between providing leadership and serving. Jesus knew all about this and modeled it perfectly.

> *Now before the Feast of the Passover, when Jesus knew that his hour had come to depart out of this world to the Father, having loved his own who were in the world, he loved them to the end. During supper, when the devil had already put it into the heart of Judas Iscariot, Simon's son, to betray him, Jesus, knowing that the Father had given all things into his hands, and that he had come from God and was going back to God, rose from supper. (John 13:1-4 (a))*

Jesus had no doubts about who He was or why He was on earth. Jesus knew where He was going and that all authority had been given to Him. He knew He was God, came from God, and was going back to His Father. Jesus never suffered from being insecure. Jesus also knew that He was the ultimate Teacher, Shepherd, and Leader. While this was a bit foggy to His followers, they had some idea of who Jesus was as well.

We read over this section of Scripture way too fast and with too much familiarity. If we would stop where I did in reading it, and use our imaginations a bit, we would be as shocked as the disciples were. As Jesus stood up many thoughts might have visited the disciples' minds, but I bet none could have guessed He was going to do what we know He did! Perhaps they thought a new teaching was coming or Jesus was going to do a miracle. Maybe they thought He forgot something and was going to go take care of it. "Is He going to multiply the food again or change the water into wine perhaps?" Many thoughts may have crossed their minds but not that He would do the unthinkable.

> *He laid aside his outer garments, and taking a towel, tied it around his waist. Then he poured water into a basin and began to wash the disciples' feet and to wipe them with the towel that was wrapped around him. He came to Simon Peter, who said to him, "Lord, do you wash my feet?" Jesus answered him, "What I am doing you do not understand now, but afterward you will understand." Peter said to him, "You shall never wash my feet." Jesus answered him, "If I do not wash you, you have no share with me." (John 13:4(b))*

Servants washed feet. John, since he was the youngest, probably should have done it but Jesus, Who was the Master, did it. None of the other disciples offered to do the necessary task either. When Jesus came to wash Peter's feet, the guy known as rock crumbled. Jesus' action was probably the reason Judas ended up acting on what Satan put into his heart. Messiah's simply do not take the role of a servant, and for Judas, he was looking for a warrior, not someone that washed feet.

Here is exactly what Jesus said after the deed:

> *When he had washed their feet and put on his outer garments and resumed his place, he said to them, "Do you understand what I have done to you? You call me Teacher and Lord, and you are right, for so I am. If I then, your Lord and Teacher, have washed your feet, you also ought to wash one*

> *another's feet. For I have given you an example, that you also should do just as I have done to you. Truly, truly, I say to you, a servant is not greater than his master, nor is a messenger greater than the one who sent him. If you know these things, blessed are you if you do them. (John 13:12-17)*

I hope someone videoed this chapter so we can view it in heaven. What a scene to watch. I would love to have seen the expression on everyone's face as Jesus resumed His place at the head of the table. "Do you understand what I have done?" Jesus asked. Of course not! These are the guys that are usually arguing about which one of *them* is the greatest. "You call me Teacher and Lord and you are right, for so I am." Jesus knew Who He was. Jesus made His point loud and clear to His men. "If I then, your Lord and Teacher, have washed your feet, you also ought to wash one another's feet." I wonder if there was tension in the room or relief. Did the men get the picture or were they in a state of shock? Perhaps they thought, "You mean I don't have to fight for my respect?" Or, "You want me to wash his feet? No way." "Humble myself the way You just did, I do not think so." That was probably Judas' response as he left to become a traitor.

Jesus set an example to be followed and it begins with leadership. These twelve men were allowed to see Deity become a lowly servant. Jesus did not leave it vague for He said, "I have given you an example, that you should also do just as I have done to you." I can imagine Jesus adding, "Got it, good. Now go do it." "In case you still wonder about this guys, a servant is not greater than his Master. I did it; you must also for you certainly are not greater than I am." Just to make sure Jesus added, "If you know these things, blessed are you if you do them." Will we be blessed in this way?

Pastors, we should be the first to offer to clean the toilets or scrub the floor. We should offer to assist with any task or service that needs doing, that is, if we are going to be like Jesus. Is there some job beneath us? Not if we are going to follow our Master's example. "Well, I have too much education to sweep floors in the church." Really, you are more educated than the One Who knows everything. "I went to school for years!" Well, Jesus created the universe. "What would people think if I knelt and cleaned up that mess on the floor?" Probably what the disciples first thought when Jesus wiped off dirty feet with His towel. However, maybe after they thought about it a bit, they might just join in serving and everyone would be better off.

Let me be transparent here, and at the risk of offending my fellow pastors, I will press on with care. Pastoring can be quite 'ego-stroking' and 'head-enlarging.' We all love to hear how wonderful we are and the sheep often praise the shepherd. Yes, there are times of conflict and pain, and we will get to that in a later chapter, but in a healthy, functioning church body, praise usually abounds. "Oh, I don't know how you do all you do," the adoring sister chirps. "It must be wonderful to be married to such a saint," our smirking spouses hear. "That was an anointed message, you must be so close to Jesus," some friend tells us. We blush, say thank you to them, and quietly whisper our gratitude for God's grace yet again. Appreciation is wonderful and needed; elevation to living sainthood is not.

I heard James Dobson say one time, "The problem with being on a pedestal is that a step in any direction is down." Wise words from a wise man. We must be careful of allowing others to idolize us for God will not share His glory, even with His under-shepherds. We are forgiven sinners that have been called and honored to serve as servants, and we must keep this in the forefront of our minds. Cleaning toilets helps us to remember who we are and Whom we serve. We are called to serve just as Jesus told us to do. We would be wise to remember and do it.

Mark

Jeff is exactly right that pastors are called to serve, and for the most part, we have only one natural enemy that constantly stalks us in an attempt to keep us from assuming the posture of a servant: our own ego. That's why I love gentle humor that is intended to keep us pastors from taking ourselves too seriously.

> One would-be poet said, "My pastor's eyes I never see shine. When he prays, he closes his, and when he preaches, I closes mine."

One woman chirped to her pastor as she left the service one day, "I declare, pastor, but every one of your sermons is better than the next one!" And one man said, with great gratitude, "My wife *loves* your sermons, pastor... especially since she lost her mind!"

I am also grateful to my wife and children who know me better than anyone in the pews or on the planet, and love me anyway. They keep my feet on the ground and my heart in the Word. They can also detect phoniness in my message within a nanosecond. I remember the *Leadership* cartoon years ago where the pastor and his wife are driving home in their Sunday best, and she is looking straight ahead with her arms folded and a grim expression, while he drives. Her husband says, "Well, everything was going fine in my sermon today until you said out loud, 'Humph!'"

Besides listening carefully to my wife's comments about my ministry, I also tune my heart to being a servant by being available to help people at their point of need, whatever that is. Jesus' example of washing the disciples feet may mean little to us if we just think in terms of dirty toes. But if there is a family moving from one house to another, try to show up and lend them a strong back and a weak mind. Make an effort to visit the shut-ins in your congregation, spending time hearing their stories and praying with them. Meet with men in the church who want to grow as fathers or young men who want counsel or direction or instruction. Invite different families and singles from the church over for a meal regularly, opening your home and your hearts to them as you break bread together, and talk about life's challenges and the Lord's blessings. These are just a few ways we pastors can wash the feet of our fellow believers.

Being a servant will undergird all we do in the ministry and will resurface in other chapters so we can move on. In the next chapter, we will look at one character trait that is critical to any pastor. In fact, the Scriptures state that this one will help produce some amazing character traits in our life if we will allow it. Every servant of God needs this one and especially the pastors, but before we discover what it is, let us pause a minute for some reflection.

Reflection Points for Pastors:

1. Do I need an ego check or deflation experience? Be honest.

2. Have I absorbed praise for myself that should have been passed on to God and others?

3. Am I willing to do the menial tasks or have I grown past that stage in my ministry?

4. Do I spend time wondering how great I am or how I can serve more?

Reflection Points: Those Who Support Them:

1. Am I a servant or someone that loves to be seen?

2. Do I use the pastor as a tool to gain approval or respect from others?

3. Am I following Jesus' example or that of the disciples?

4. What are my expectations of my pastor - servant or saint?

4 Called to Endure

Not only that, but we rejoice in our sufferings, knowing that suffering produces endurance, and endurance produces character, and character produces hope, and hope does not put us to shame, because God's love has been poured into our hearts through the Holy Spirit who has been given to us. (Romans 5:3-5)

Jeff

Endurance is defined in a typical dictionary as the act, quality, or power of withstanding hardship or stress and/or the state or fact of persevering. Sounds like a pastor to me! Many pastors are underpaid and have a large amount of stress. Consider Paul's comments in this passage:

Are they Hebrews? So am I. Are they Israelites? So am I. Are they offspring of Abraham? So am I. Are they servants of Christ? I am a better one—I am talking like a madman—with far greater labors, far

> *more imprisonments, with countless beatings, and often near death. Five times I received at the hands of the Jews the forty lashes less one. Three times I was beaten with rods. Once I was stoned. Three times I was shipwrecked; a night and a day I was adrift at sea; on frequent journeys, in danger from rivers, danger from robbers, danger from my own people, danger from Gentiles, danger in the city, danger in the wilderness, danger at sea, danger from false brothers; in toil and hardship, through many a sleepless night, in hunger and thirst, often without food, in cold and exposure. And, apart from other things, there is the daily pressure on me of my anxiety for all the churches. Who is weak, and I am not weak? Who is made to fall, and I am not indignant? (2 Corinthians 11:22-29)*

Paul was a superman for evangelism and church planting, and he was a pastor at heart. Paul hurt when others hurt and this is the calling of a pastor. In his defense as an apostle, Paul gives us just a glimpse of what every pastor knows. "...There is the daily pressure on me of anxiety for all the churches. Who is weak, and I am not weak?" Paul felt the pain of real people personally, and so do most pastors. We hurt when those we love and serve suffer.

One of our jobs is to listen to people's pain and to pray for them. Rarely will someone come up to me and say, "Hi pastor, just wanted you to know I love my wife and kids, and I am doing great." Most times, we tend to hear, "Can I talk to you for a minute." We know the look and we know that it will not be a minute. Something is wrong and many times, very wrong. We listen, pray, cry and hurt as we find out what has happened to someone we love.

Funerals, marriage counseling, reading angry or hurtful letters, hospital visits, refereeing leadership or staff meetings, and a host of other events all take a toll on our emotional lives. Most pastors do not complain about that for that is what we are called to do, but that does not reduce the emotional wear and tear. Paul said there was daily pressure from the churches he loved and he was correct. We hurt because we care and when we cease to hurt, we should probably move into some other line of work.

Another enjoyable part of my world is hanging out with men. Over the last thirty years, I have met with many brothers and it is interesting to note that almost all of them suffer with the same problem. If you guessed lust, you are partially correct, but that is not the only one we all battle. Most men begin a conversation like this, "I don't know, I just wonder what it is all about. I do not really feel like I am doing anything of value. I get up, go to work, come home, try to be a good husband and father, go to bed, get up, go to work, it's the same routine and what is it all for?" In short, they are asking the same question we all struggle with — does my life have meaning? Pastors are not immune to this struggle regardless of how "successful" they may appear.

I cannot prove it, but I bet at the bottom of many of the endless church building campaigns is the desire to leave something behind after the pastor is dead or moves on. No one wants to feel like their life did not really matter, and pastors are the same. All the sermons, all the meetings, all the pain — did it really mean anything? Did the investment of our lives really matter to anyone long term? What most pastors struggle with is the lack of closure or completion.

I have friends that are in construction, we drive to a place, and they show me the work of their hands. What can pastors show beyond the brick and mortar they built? How do you measure the impact of a sermon or counseling session? Our job description is to equip the saints so they can go do the work. We are told to teach, disciple, pray for, and love those under our care. How do you measure the effectiveness of those activities? Few of us have enough of a long-term view to evaluate the work of our lives, but there is One who does, and for that, I am grateful. God knows. God keeps track and God rewards His faithful servants, no matter the size of the work they may do for Him. God measures in faithfulness, not numbers, or worldly accomplishments.

Upon entering the full-time ministry, an older pastor took me aside and said, "Son, the occupational hazard of the ministry is discouragement and disillusionment with people." At the ripe old age of 25, I did not have a clue what this seasoned pastor knew quite well. The pastor had seen a great deal of the dark side of those two words in his life and most of us in the ministry eventually will as well. Pastors struggle with discouragement and steps must be taken to battle this reality. If we are unprepared for the battle, we will not know how to fight and win.

Studies have been performed and they usually reveal that the majority of pastors, up to 90% will not finish well. While sin issues, relationship problems, health failure knock out a few, by the far the biggest cause is becoming discouraged and disillusioned. I have not performed the research but I think it would be safe to say that the majority of pastors that quit do so on Mondays.

For me Mondays are always the hardest. It is probably the emotional letdown after the Sunday service, but for the first several years of my church plant, I dusted off my résumé every Monday morning. Without fail, I would check online to see if there was something, anything that I could do instead of being a pastor. Every time I found something interesting, I had a check from the Lord, but that did not stop me from looking! Mondays were rough for me. Maybe they are fine for you, but you probably can relate to the feelings I struggled with early on in the ministry. Thoughts like:

- Why am I doing this again?
- Well, that certainly did not work well.
- That illustration bombed.
- So many people sleeping they must be bored.
- No one said anything about the message today.

Throw in a critical comment or nasty email and I was ready to bolt.

I have grown up some since the early days and I rarely dust off the résumé, but discouragement still visits. Feeling unappreciated or unloved can trigger half a day's worth of downtime. Wondering why we keep plugging away after yet another family leaves in a huff, still comes around now and again. "You are our favorite pastor. We love you and your vision...but we feel led to move along." Most pastors will smile at that comment, but inside we struggle with rejection, wondering where we failed, what we could have, or should have done differently. Most of us care deeply when someone leaves our church. We cannot help but take it personally, even when it is not.

We are called to endure and to walk in the footsteps of our Master. There are far too many verses to list but just consider these samples for a moment:

> *For it has been granted to you that for the sake of Christ you should not only believe in him but also suffer for his sake. (Philippians 1:29)*

> *Share in suffering as a good soldier of Christ Jesus. (2 Timothy 2:3)*

> *For what credit is it if, when you sin and are beaten for it, you endure? But if when you do good and suffer for it you endure, this is a gracious thing in the sight of God. (1 Peter 2:20)*

We will most likely not be called upon to endure all that Christ or Paul did, but we will still suffer. Paul said it had been *granted to us* to suffer, which implies a wonderful gift, something of real value. Paul tells his young disciple Timothy that soldiers will share in sufferings — it is just part of the duty of being in the war. Peter even went so far as to say that it is a gracious thing to suffer unjustly, if we endure it well. Thanks, Peter!

The presupposition under the verse I opened this chapter with is that suffering is normal. But even beyond being normal, it is purposeful. Suffering produces endurance and endurance is a fundamental requirement for pastors and every believer. As we learn to endure, we develop stronger character and from that strength comes hope that cannot be shaken. Suffering is a good thing for us, even if it is very unpleasant. God gives us the grace to embrace suffering to end up having hope.

Because we learn how to develop hope, we will be effective for the Kingdom until Jesus moves us on to either eternity or out of the ministry to some other work. Our lives and ministry matter greatly and to a large number of people. Our sermons, service projects, counseling, books, and even our buildings, do influence many. We may not grasp the fruit of our labors, but as I said before, God does; and He keeps excellent records. If Jesus said that when we even give a cup of water in His name we would not lose our reward, then He knows how to weigh the value of our lives properly.

Your study time in the Word of God, prayers that only God hears, turning the other cheek when you wanted to strike back, hours of frustration on seemingly endless phone calls, and a host of other labors of love, are being recorded. God knows and He fully appreciates your efforts even if no one else ever does. God alone understands the eternal value of your services so do not become overly discouraged if you, or others, do not. We are called to be faithful, endure and to develop character that leads to hope; we can do that much!

Mark

I agree with Jeff that one of the greatest struggles of any pastor is with discouragement. It is easy to see why, as the job of the leaders of every church will be examined by God one day! The writer of Hebrews exhorted the church to "Obey your leaders and submit to them, for they are keeping watch over your souls, as those who will have to give an account." (Hebrews 13:17) I want to suggest to pastors that we need to teach our people how to encourage the leaders, because many times they honestly do not know how to do that. That's one reason why Hebrews 13 is in the Bible. That's also why Paul gives us this strong exhortation in

> "We ask you, brothers, to respect those who labor among you and are over you in the Lord and admonish you, and to esteem them very highly in love because of their work." (1 Thessalonians 5:12-13)

Now, that verse is a two-edge sword, isn't it, pastor? We must teach our people to respect those who labor, lead, and work. But that means that they must see *us* working!

I would suggest two ways a congregation can encourage its leaders. First, come alongside them to help any way you can, with words of encouragement, with prayers, and even with physical help. I am reminded of good friends of mine who are missionaries in Kenya. They decided in 2005 to tackle Mount Kilimanjaro, which is the tallest freestanding mountain in the world, at 19,500 feet. Larry and Mary Warren spent seven days climbing that mountain, but they almost didn't make it. The last day of the climb was to begin at 10 p.m. and end the next afternoon at the summit. Larry asked why they would be climbing in the dark, not able to see where they were going. The guide answered, "Because if you could see where you were going, you would not climb!"

With only five hours to go to the summit, the guide had to make a decision. Some in the group were slowing the others down. "I will separate the group into two, so that you can all keep up your pace and get to the top." Larry said the guide separated the 12 climbers into a group of 10, and a group of two: Larry and Mary! Seems they were slowing down the pack just a bit. Two guides remained with Larry and Mary, and the others raced ahead toward the summit. Larry said that the last five hours were grueling, and he was praying that Mary would quit so he could quit with her. Finally, with three hours left, Mary was done. "I can't go any further," she said to the guides. "Can you go for 30 more minutes?" the guide asked. Mary agreed she could, thinking that the summit was a half-hour away. "He used that same line about five more times!" Larry said, but it worked to keep them motivated and moving.

With only an hour to go to the top, Mary was completely worn out. That's when the guides did for the Warrens what every leader needs when it feels like we cannot go on. Larry said, "One went in front of us and Mary held onto his backpack. The second went behind her, pushing her on the back, and I came behind the second guide and held on as these men literally pushed and pulled us up the mountain! Yes, we kept walking ... we did our part ... we did the best we could, but it was the strength and determination of these experienced guides that helped us make it to the top."

All of us in church leadership need people who will give us a push or a pull to get through difficult times. But there's a second, even more practical way that a congregation can encourage its leaders.

Many times, the greatest source of stress in a pastor's life can be financial. Alistair Begg gave a talk at a pastors' conference years ago entitled, "Dealing with the Blues." His subject was ministerial depression, and the auditorium was packed with discouraged pastors and elders. After the session, elders from one church asked to talk with Alistair in private. "Our problem is not with the pastor, but his wife," they said. "She is deeply depressed and we have tried everything, but nothing has helped. What should we do?" Pastor Begg said, "Increase your pastor's annual salary by $5,000." The elders were shocked and had no response. Later, one of the members of the church who had heard about this conversation found Alistair and said, "You don't know how right on target you were. Our pastor's wife has never been able to buy new shoes for her children, and the elders wear it as a badge of honor that the pastor's family has to scrape together pennies to make ends meet. They believe they are helping them trust God. They think they are helping the pastor never to become a lover of money by making sure he doesn't have any money to love."

Does your pastor or his wife have the blues? Make sure it's not because they are being unfairly compensated for their work in God's church.

There are several distinct stages of ministry that we will look at in the next chapter but before we move on let us spend a few minutes musing.

Reflection Point for Pastors:

1. What do I think of when the word endurance is considered regarding pastoring?

2. Do I have a biblical view of suffering?

3. How do I move from discouragement to being enthused again in God?

4. If our enemy cannot get us to fail, he will get us to spend too much time being consumed with what only God really can know. Is that a true sentence? How does that apply to me?

Reflection Points: Those Who Support Them:

1. Have you ever thought about your pastor being discouraged?

2. What could you do to assist them with this ongoing battle of relevance?

3. If you have been part of the problem, what can you do to change that to become part of the solution?

4. How could you help your pastor this week?

5 The Stages of Ministry

The glory of young men is their strength, but the splendor of old men is their gray hair. (Proverbs 20:29)

Jeff

I think God has a sense of humor. When we are younger, we often possess tremendous strength but not enough wisdom to use it properly. By the time we gain the wisdom, we do not have the strength or energy left. Youthful zeal has caused some major problems and conquered almost the entire world. How old was Alexander the Great when he amassed one of the largest armies of the ancient world? Oh yes, he was thirty. Jesus was thirty and so was David when they reached to the apex of their "fame." Priests were supposed to retire at fifty and young men served in the army, not the older ones. "We are the Lord's army," goes the old song many of us sung as children. Young children love to march and ride, but older soldiers tend to like to observe from a safer position. There is a reason the military drafts eighteen year olds and not those over thirty or forty.

As pastors, many tend to enter into the ministry at a younger age and sometimes stay beyond when they should retire. As newer pastors we are often full of zeal and vision, and as older ones, sometimes we end up full of bitterness, cynicism and regrets. Part of the problem is of course dashed expectations, and another part is not having a proper understanding of the various stages of ministry.

The Birth

We looked at the calling into ministry in the first chapter and I will label that the "birth" season. We begin a new way of life when we enter into the pastorate. It does not really matter if we are the senior guy or the youngest on the staff, life will never be the same. Being a pastor is a wonderful mix of excitement, joy, pleasure, and pain. We love serving the Lord and helping people and many times those same people can inflict great emotional damage.

Our baptism into ministry may come in many fashions or through varied events, but we almost all start out full of zeal and enthusiasm looking forward to God moving through us. However, like our first birth, there are often some growing pains and a great deal to master. Learning how to work on or with a staff, a leadership team, church boards, volunteers, and the general public, are all challenging to a new pastor. Counseling, study and prayer habits, and people's expectations all play a role. "You're a pastor and you drive like that?" "You watched that movie?" People rightfully expect us to be different because we are pastors. Maybe that is unfair but those expectations must be handled.

We all make mistakes as new pastors. Okay, we still make them as older pastors, but not the same ones. For example in my early days:

- I was teaching on circumcision and backed myself into an embarrassing verbal corner with the illustration.
- I asked someone I did not know if they were visiting the church. They replied rather curtly, "No, we have been here eighteen years sitting in the same seats."
- I called someone repeatedly by the wrong name.
- I misquoted Scripture, misapplied texts, used improper illustrations, took passages out of context, and basically did great violence to the pulpit with my bad habits.
- I stunk at hospital calls and was not very good at counseling either.

In general terms, I was young, arrogant, a smart aleck know-it-all, not very kind, and rather selfish. The good news is that God still used me and has helped me to see some of the blind spots that were so clear to many others. God does not demand perfection, for only Jesus is perfect. What God does want is humility and someone who will walk in obedience. Just because we start out being rough or on the wrong foot does not mean we need to finish poorly. Sadly, the reverse is also true. Many start well and end in shame and disgrace.

Churches, like pastors have a beginning stage. All churches began somewhere at some time with a purpose of some sort. It is easier to begin a new work and grow together through the birth pains, than it is to take over an established church. No matter how you assume the position of pastor, you will go through a birth stage. That's where your pastoral life begins.

The Growth Stage

If we survive the birth stage, which was a narrow escape for me, we eventually settle into a growth pattern. We may or may not see numerical growth of those who follow us, but we all should see spiritual maturity develop in our own lives.

WARNING - planned tirade coming, please skip the next two paragraphs if you do not want to endure it.

Numerical growth is somewhat a misnomer, and highly overrated. Most church growth is typically transfer growth because people move from one church to the next faster than they trade used cars. I was the administrator of a church of 3,500 people that suffered through the senior pastor's immoral failure. Over 2,000 people left that church and ended up going to a little church of about 150 people. That church of course exploded with growth that caused an explosion of buildings and hiring of new pastors. Was there real growth, or just a transfer of sheep to a new sheep shed? I am not discounting the work that the new church was doing; I am just using this as an example of how people move around from church to church.

Most mega churches are full of transfer growth, not new converts. This is not evil or necessarily bad, but it often leads to the small church pastor feeling like a failure because they only have ninety people. In fact, the vast majority of churches have around ninety people. It is a shame the pastor is tempted to feel unsuccessful, because the small church pastor is a key to spreading the Gospel and helping millions of people. The mega-church pastor often gets the highest praise from man, but I think God has a special place for the small church pastor. For what's it worth, keep up the good work pastor and do not buy the trap of comparison to others! Okay, end of personal tirade about numbers; we now rejoin the chapter already in progress...

By personal growth in our pastoring, I am referring to not only avoiding the repetition of the mistakes made in the early days, but also moving into actually implementing our vision. God called us and gave us something to do for Him. It is during this season of our ministry life that we should be seeing the impartation of that vision to others. Regardless of the vision we were given, we want to share it and see it adopted by as many people as possible.

My vision and passion is for the restoration of the family. Yours may be reaching the lost, a foreign people group, inner-city children, the homeless, or singles, but we all want to see others join us in our vision and passion. It is during this phase of ministry that we build and focus on the vision. God spoke something to us and now we lay the foundation and begin to build the structure, and we will work on the building until we leave.

During the growth process, the vision is refined and shared with anyone that will listen to us. We usually begin our ministry with a vague sense of what we want to accomplish but as the years roll along, the passion becomes clearer and more defined. In my church, we began with a number of negatives and not too many positives. We would state, "We are not going to have this type ministry." In addition, "We won't be doing this, that, and the other." We knew a great deal of what we were not going to do and not too much of what we should be doing.

Sometime in the first few years, we moved to a much more pro-active approach. We changed from, "We are not going to do this and that," to "This is why we exist." We clarified what we wanted to see happen in people's lives, and figured out more effective ways to accomplishing it. We established a formal vision statement and began to organize our ministry around it. Growth and maturity followed as we clarified why we existed.

Part of the growth that takes place is also personal. During this stage, we begin to settle into our calling. Yes, there are struggles, and sometimes they are very difficult, but we know we are supposed to be doing what we are doing. My illustration to explain this is what I call "Driving a Stake." If I am convinced that God told me to be in the ministry then I drive a stake or tent peg in the ground of my heart and mind. If I know that this was God, I am sure of it, I cannot be talked out of it, then, I beat that stake deep into the ground and attach a tether line to it. I am connected to that stake come what may. When the fog comes and I cannot see I pull the line. Still attached. When the storms of opposition hit and I feel like quitting I look back at the stake. At times, I feel like running away, but I know God told me to do this so I stay. A firmly placed stake will help us when we are tempted to give up. God is not confused or fickle. If He told us something, He will empower us to accomplish it. We will not quit until God tells us to.

As we grow into our calling, we continue to learn. Maybe we complete some more academic pursuits or maybe we learn how to study better. We are always learners for we never arrive at completion. We must grow into the place where we are comfortable with who we are. We do not have to know everything; we simply need to know the One who does. Those who follow us are looking to us for leadership, not because we are God, but most likely because of our vision. Our job is to point them to God. When they ask us something we do not know, we tell them so, and then we go find out if we can. We disciple, we do not become deity to others. God alone is God; we are just His servants called to assist others in the process of knowing Him.

This stage consumes the bulk of our ministerial lives. We have an entrance point into ministry that I referred to as the birth, and it really does not matter how old we are chronologically. Shortly after the initial stage, we quickly learn from our youthful mistakes and settle down into our growth stage. This stage will last until we die or leave the ministry pre-death and will overlap with the final stage of our ministry life. Again, age is not necessarily the issue, but it will play a part. For example, a man that I have known for over twenty years showed up one day at my church about eight years ago. Shocked, I asked him why he was there and his reply was humorous and insightful. He patted me on the cheek and said, "Well, now that you are older you finally have something worth listening to." I could have chosen to be insulted for I have always had something worth listening to, or I could do what I did, which was to laugh and agree. He was of course correct. My children were all grown at the time and I was rapidly approaching fifty years of age. What I knew at this age was indeed better than what I knew in my twenties. Age does that.

Mentor

As we age and mature, the final stage of our ministry will overlap the previous one. We will always keep maturing and growing until we leave this life, at least we should. However, the cold reality of fleeting youth eventually creeps into our lives. The truth of my age hit me one time when I was playing softball with a bunch of men. I played shortstop and a routine ground ball was heading towards me. I bent over and attempted to catch the ball. In my mind, the glove was on the ground, and placed perfectly. Reality however was realized when the ball went into the outfield and everyone was laughing. I thought the glove was down on the ground, but was really by my knees. It turns out that my back and legs were acting independently of my mind. I had indeed, "lost a step."

This is not all bad, even though our egos tend to be bruised. Younger folks get up and give us their seats and we begin to receive cash discounts when we eat out. What we also do is begin to contemplate the end. When we are young, we think we are immortal but as we age, we realize that our lives are a vapor. Years seem to fly by and before you know it, there is less ahead than behind. As we approach late middle age, which is a shifting term I know, we begin to analyze what is ahead and what is behind. My dear wife loves to tease me with this truth. We were sitting together one morning having our cup of coffee and she blurts out, "You know Jeff, in fifteen years you are going to be seventy." Now what would possess someone to say something so cruel!

My wife's comments, while hard to come to grips with, are true. At fifty-five then, there were fifteen years left until seventy, and there are even fewer now. At seventy, many significant changes are inevitable. Physical limitations follow age. Even with good health, there are not many seventy-year-old star athletes. There are not many pastors either. We must begin to look forward for the sake of the vision that God has given to us. Who is going to take the mantle? Who is going to carry it on when we are unable?

The mentoring stage of our ministry is both looking forward and backward. We look to whom we can invest in to carry on our life's message and we look back to remember what we have learned. Victories and mistakes are excellent teachers, if we will learn from them. We can pass on, no; we must pass on each one on to the next generation, if we do not want to disappear from history, or memory. I am what I am today because of what other, older people shared with me. I had personal relationships with older men and women and I have read a great deal of what people from previous generations have written. Both have helped me grow.

We need those older than us to help us. We, who are quickly becoming older, need to be willing to help others. It is not all about us, in fact, it never has been; it is all about Jesus. Older pastors need to build into their schedule time for younger ones. We must impart to the generation following what we have learned. We should write books and blogs. We should record our messages and use the technologies available to spread them around everywhere we can. We have a responsibility to others to share what we have learned, for this is God's method to keep the message going generationally.

Mark

One of the verses I had to memorize when I traveled with an evangelistic team in the 1980's was Psalm 37:25, "I have been young, and now am old, yet I have not seen the righteous forsaken or his children begging for bread." I was 26 years old when I memorized that verse and had no idea in practical terms what it meant. Thirty years, seven children, and three grandchildren later, I understand it a lot better. God is faithful. He takes care of His people, and He leads His undershepherds along, every step of the way. I am in the mentor stage now, as Jeff puts it, and God has given me opportunities to help younger men get a vision for ministry. I hope it is part of His plan to give me many more years of mentoring before I am led out to pasture.

In the birth stage, I made every mistake that is possible for a pastor to make, and then I made each one of them again for good measure. One of my most embarrassing moments in the pulpit happened in the first year or two as I was passionately preaching about Lot's steady slouch toward Sodom. You remember, right? Lot pitched his tents toward Sodom. Then he moved into Sodom. Finally, Sodom moved into him and the result was that he could not even save all of his family when the fire from heaven was about to fall. But if you try to say "Lot pitched his tents toward Sodom," and you transpose some of the sounds, it can sound almost pornographic. Needless to say, my face turned bright red, and I couldn't even look at my wife's.

That was a rookie mistake that harmed no one, and we will all have them. My greater mistakes, however, walked into the church right along with my immaturity in knowing how to lead people. I drove more than I led. I scolded more than I instructed. I shamed when I should have exhorted.

It was during the first year of my ministry at Antioch that one of the elders suggested that I find a pastor in the community to mentor me. He suggested a man by the name of Howard Thompson who was the pastor of Burlington Assembly of God. I called him and asked if I could meet with him to learn how to be a pastor and he said yes. In fact, he invited me to come to his office the very next week and said that his secretary would have lunch for us. That started a friendship that continues to this day, and for more than five years, I met with Pastor Thompson every week for lunch. There were a few other pastors who joined us at various times along the way, but most of the time it was just Howard and me. I learned so much from him.

I would come in most weeks with a new challenge that was going on in the church, and Howard always had words of encouragement, Scripture, and a good story from his own experience to make me laugh and help me see my way clear. He told me one time when I was dealing with a cantankerous member, "When you preach, don't throw the corn cob at that old ram out there. He is likely to duck and you will end up hurting the lamb sitting right behind him." Great advice for a young preacher who knew how to slip an illustration in that was honed to a point and intended to wound rather than encourage!

Every young pastor needs a Howard Thompson to walk with him through those first few years, and every older pastor needs to *be* a Howard Thompson for someone else.

I wrote this column for the newspaper last year upon Howard's retirement from the pastorate:

Thank you, Pastor Thompson

If you ask Howard Thompson why he wears cowboy boots with his suit, he'll tell you about growing up in Stigler, Oklahoma. But if you ask him about his passion in life, he will tell you about being a pastor. On January 26, Howard Thompson will preach his last sermon as pastor of Burlington Assembly, where he has served for 42 years. On his watch, the church has grown in number and influence, and their outreach to the community now includes the Caring Kitchen (which serves the homeless and hungry on the weekends), the Assembly Oaks Retirement Community, and Burlington Christian Academy. Pastor Thompson also achieved the rank of Colonel as the long-time Chaplain for the Burlington Police Department. Many would regard him as "Burlington's pastor."

When Howard Thompson was called into the ministry as a senior in high school, his pastor gave him a chance to preach his first sermon. "I was very shy, and not much of a public speaker," Thompson recalls. "So, the first time I tried to preach, I fainted." Undeterred, he enrolled in Bible College in Springfield, Missouri after graduation. It was there that Howard Thompson realized his call to be a pastor. A group of students cleaned up an abandoned building and started a ministry, which soon became a church and in his second year as a student, Howard became the pastor. "Just imagine having a teenager as your pastor," Howard said. "They put up with a lot. But I realized that I loved every bit of pastoral ministry: visiting the people, going to the hospitals, preaching, and teaching." In many ways, he has embodied Peter's advice to those in ministry to "shepherd the flock of God that is among you, exercising oversight."

One of the most gratifying things for Pastor Thompson has been watching families grow in the Lord through the years. "To marry two young people, then dedicate their children, watch those children grow up in the Lord and then to be able to participate in their weddings. What a blessing. To see that come full circle has given me great fulfillment. I know many fine pastors who haven't been able to stay long enough to see that. They have missed a great blessing."

I often think back 25 years to a time in my own ministry when I met with Howard Thompson every week for lunch. He was a mentor to me early on, and I am forever grateful. I asked Pastor Thompson what advice he would give to young pastors today. He said, "First, be sure of the call. Ministry is not a profession; it is a calling. Second, remember that your relationship with the Lord is your first priority. Third, endeavor to do what the Lord wants you to do. Be faithful."

Howard remembers a time as a young pastor when he was working to set some trusses on a new church building. A freak wind came up and blew him and the trusses to the ground. Howard was not hurt, but he was heartbroken about it, and went back to his little office and cried out to God: "I thought you cared about churches. You could have stopped that wind. I thought you called me to plant a church. Don't you care?" When Howard ran out of steam, he said he heard the Lord speak to his heart. "Son, I did call you. And I care about building churches. But right now, I'm trying to build Myself a man."

I believe the Lord built a fine one in Howard Thompson. Thank you, Pastor, for your faithful ministry.

You can hear the interview I did with Pastor Thompson for my podcast at http://www.healthychurchradio.com/hcr047-a-veteran-pastor-looks-back/

Whatever stage of ministry we find ourselves in, we are primarily in the sheep tending business. I heard someone once say that God called us sheep, and He was not being complimentary. After all the years of pastoring, I would tend to agree. We will have strong sheep, weak sheep, gentle ones, and some that have very sharp teeth. In fact, most pastors at some stage of their life will suffer through a sheep mauling or two. Attack sheep in packs can be brutal. Before we move on into further discussion about sheep however, let us pause a bit and reflect.

Reflection Points for Pastors:

1. Have I driven a stake deep in the ground of my heart and mind? Is it strongly embedded to withstand the inevitable storms of ministry?

2. Do I have any older pastors in my life that I can look to as a mentor? If not, why not?

3. What stage of my ministry am I in? Is it time to move on into the next one?

4. It has been stated that you are not successful unless you have a successor. Do I have one?

Reflection Points: Those Who Support Them:

1. What stage would you say your pastor is in?

2. How can you pray for, and help them in this stage of ministry?

3. Are you someone that your pastor can trust and depend on? Why or why not?

4. Do you have expectations of your pastor that are unrealistic?

6 Strong Sheep, Weak Sheep

I would be an excellent pastor if it were not for all these people.

Jeff

Jesus is the Good Shepherd and we pastors are trying to follow His example. Jesus taught the people when they needed it, loved them, corrected them, led them, and laid down His life for them. We must do the same if we are to be good and faithful servants.

Once, a fellow pastor of mine attended a motivation seminar in our city. He came back pumped up and ready to change his church. The speaker used many military terms and he really whipped up the crowd. Change would happen in these churches and it would happen right now if the pastors would just be forceful enough. The first Sunday back my pastor friend stated something along these lines — "I am sick and tired of pastoring privates, I want to lead generals. If you can't step up and be an officer then I don't want you here." As most older pastors can imagine, the reaction was swift and decisive. The next week the church was much smaller, and eventually died. What went wrong? Why could no one see the wisdom of these words? Who wants to work with privates when becoming officers is the goal?

Let's try another illustration. Most leaders know that people do not like, or respond well to dramatic changes. The old adage is to make five degree turns not ninety degree ones. Why? Because people are sheep, and sharp turns usually result in a good deal of crashes. Sheep are led and not driven like cattle. Gentle turns and slow grazing works far better than rushed meals on a roller coaster. Many people simply view change as bad and if rushed into it, very bad. A wise pastor learns to lead, not command, and demand.

Jesus often taught in parables and answered many questions with questions. Why? In addition to separating those who were serious from those who were not, He knew that self-discovery is far better than having everything spoon-fed. When a group of people gradually sees the truth and wisdom of a path, they take it without much fuss. When it is demanded of them to walk on that path, revolts often ensue. Pastors lead — they do not drive. Pastors teach and explain why; they do not demand and command instant obedience, at least not the effective ones.

The truth is that in any church regardless of size, there will be both strong sheep and weak ones. The pastor must learn to deal with both of them. I know this section of Scripture is geared to those under the Old Covenant, and could better be applied to kings and rulers, but pastors can learn a great deal from the truth in Ezekiel 34:

The word of the LORD came to me: "Son of man, prophesy against the shepherds of Israel; prophesy and say to them: 'This is what the Sovereign LORD says: Woe to the shepherds of Israel who only take care of themselves! Should not shepherds take care of the flock? (Ezekiel 34:1-2 NIV)

The last thing most of us want to hear from the mouth of God begins with, "Woe." As Ezekiel, speaking for the Lord, rebukes the shepherds in this chapter, we would be wise to listen and learn. The first two verses show us where our focus should be and where it should not rest. We are commanded by God, as His under-shepherds, to take care of the sheep and not just ourselves. Of course, we must take care of ourselves, but not at the expense of the flock. We are not called to fleece the flock but to love and lay down our lives for them. How were those shepherds doing this? The prophet explains crisply:

You eat the fat, you clothe yourselves with the wool, you slaughter the fat ones, but you do not feed the sheep. (Ezekiel 34:3)

The sheep were being used to take care of the needs of the shepherd instead of the other way around. These shepherds were eating the sheep instead of making sure the sheep had enough food. The sheep were being slaughtered so the shepherds could stay warm. Shepherds are given to the flock to lead and protect it, not to be consumed by them!

The rebukes are not finished yet:

The weak you have not strengthened, the sick you have not healed, the injured you have not bound

> *up, the strayed you have not brought back, the lost you have not sought, and with force and harshness you have ruled them. (Ezekiel 34:5)*

Ouch. Five different categories of pastoral ministry are included in just this one verse. Did you see them? First, there are always going to be weak sheep. Not all sheep will become generals or leaders. In fact, some will always struggle, just barely making if from one day to the next. Second, there will be sick sheep. Some from physical illness others from mental and emotional ones. Third, there will be injured sheep for sheep often trample on one another and sometimes stomp pretty hard. Fourth, there will be strays, and fifth, some will even end up lost. Shepherds learn to love and live with all five types of sheep, that is, if they want to be like Jesus. Oh, the last part of that verse is pretty pointed as well; you ruled them with force and harshness and that is not acceptable.

Yes, we are to give double honor to those that rule well as Paul stated in 1 Timothy 5:17, but Jesus also taught that the leadership principles of the Kingdom are servant based. We rule well when we serve most. Shepherds lead; they do not cajole, manipulate, intimidate, or "Lord it over" their flock with fear or anger.

What was the result of the shepherds failing to be godly leaders for the flock under their care? Ezekiel paints the picture:

> *So they were scattered, because there was no shepherd, and they became food for all the wild beasts. My sheep were scattered; they wandered over all the mountains and on every high hill. My sheep were scattered over all the face of the earth, with none to search or seek for them. (Ezekiel 34:5-6)*

The shepherds failed and the sheep paid the price. I am not a sheepherder but I know enough about the animals to know they are not the brightest creatures on the planet. They eat poison weeds, wander off cliffs, cannot really back up so they often are entangled into thorn bushes, and become lost very easily. They need tending and if the shepherds fail in the job, the sheep pay. Not all is lost in this story because God steps in. While not a pretty picture for the shepherds, the sheep have great hope. First, consider God's words to the worthless shepherds.

> *"Therefore, you shepherds, hear the word of the LORD: As I live, declares the Lord GOD, surely because my sheep have become a prey, and my sheep have become food for all the wild beasts, since there was no shepherd, and because my shepherds have not searched for my sheep, but the shepherds have fed themselves, and have not fed my sheep, therefore, you shepherds, hear the word of the LORD: Thus says the Lord GOD, Behold, I am against the shepherds, and I will require my sheep at their hand and put a stop to their feeding the sheep. No longer shall the shepherds feed themselves. I will rescue my sheep from their mouths, that they may not be food for them: (Ezekiel 34:7-10)*

"I am against the shepherds" is not encouraging, especially if the one saying it is God. God also will hold the shepherds responsible for the damage that has taken place at the hands of the worthless leaders. Wow, not something that we want to experience.

The next six verses are very encouraging for the leaderless sheep, for God Himself will do the five things that the former shepherds did not accomplish. God will seek out the lost and strays. He will bring healing to the hurting and excellent pasture to the hungry. God will help the weak sheep for God will take care of His own in spite of the failures of the leadership, and that is good news.

"Wait," states the stuttering pastor, "you do not understand because the sheep in my church can be a real pain." After pastoring for over thirty years, I would respectfully disagree with you; I do understand. More importantly, God understands as well. People can be a problem to deal with, but God gives the shepherds grace. We must learn how to act like Jesus to those under our care, even the tough ones. Jesus never gives up, and neither should we. God can and will straighten out the sheep that need adjusting, and sometimes He is the only One who can.

While God is rebuking the shepherds, restoring, and healing the weak sheep, He also has some harsh words for the selfish, self-willed, dominating, controlling, heavy-handed, control freak sheep. Okay, He did not use all those words and what He actually said was, "Fat and strong sheep," but I just wanted you to know that I know that there are some pretty nasty sheep out there. This is what God actually said:

> *"As for you, my flock, thus says the Lord God: Behold, I judge between sheep and sheep, between rams and male goats. Is it not enough for you to feed on the good pasture, that you must tread down with your feet the rest of your pasture; and to drink of clear water, that you must muddy the rest of the water with your feet? And must my sheep eat what you have trodden with your feet, and drink what you have muddied with your feet? "Therefore, thus says the Lord God to them: Behold, I, I myself*

> *will judge between the fat sheep and the lean sheep. Because you push with side and shoulder, and thrust at all the weak with your horns, till you have scattered them abroad, I will rescue my flock; they shall no longer be a prey. And I will judge between sheep and sheep. (Ezekiel 34:17-22)*

God will judge between sheep and since He does not make errors, He will do it correctly. God alone knows all of the facts and details of each life and He alone is in the proper place to judge accurately. Our job as under-shepherds is to love the weak sheep, and bear with and endure the strong ones. We must learn how to lead both types and I will address some ideas in a later chapter on how to view strong, gifted, talented, and even pushy sheep.

Mark

I wrote about our sheepishness as followers of Christ in my book, *Family-Integrated Church* in 2006. Here's an excerpt from the chapter I entitled, "What's the Big Deal about Elders?"-- USA Today carried this story on July 8, 2005.

> ISTANBUL, Turkey – "First one sheep jumped to its death. Then stunned Turkish shepherds, who had left the herd to graze while they had breakfast, watched as nearly 1,500 others followed, each leaping off the same cliff, Turkish media reported.
>
> In the end, 450 dead animals lay on top of one another in a billowy white pile, the Aksam newspaper

> said. Those who jumped later were saved as the pile got higher and the fall more cushioned.
>
> After one of the sheep tried to jump a ravine, the rest of the flock followed.
>
> 'There's nothing we can do. They're all wasted,' Nevzat Bayhan, a member of one of 26 families whose sheep were grazing in the herd, was quoted as saying..."[9]

What is going on here? You have heard the mythical story, perhaps, of lemmings rushing to the sea, committing suicide en masse. Here we have a similar story, only this time it is a herd of sheep, all following a leader who is very confused. This rogue sheep made a deadly decision and 1,500 of his closest friends blindly followed him.

You could "spin" this story and say that 450 of the sheep laid down their lives for their comrades. But don't pull the wool over your eyes. That's not what happened here.

You could say that sheep are naturally sociable and would rather die together than live alone. That, too, would be wrong, and I would be fleecing you to even suggest it.

You could say that since these sheep lived in Turkey, perhaps they thought they could fly. That would be a really "baaad" attempt at humor, and it, too, would be off the mark.

No, these sheep were simply acting the way God designed them. Sheep are not the brightest of four-legged creatures, they are defenseless, and they do tend to be followers. Hence, sheep desperately need a shepherd.

Maybe that's why God compares us to sheep in the Bible. He says in Isaiah 53:6, "All we like sheep have gone astray; we have turned -- every one -- to his own way..." Sheep, if left

---

[9] http://usatoday30.usatoday.com/news/offbeat/2005-07-08-sheep-suicide_x.htm

unattended, will wander off. A sheep can wander over a cliff or into a thicket where he is held fast, or stumble over rocks and end up 'cast' (on his back, unable to turn). In any of these scenarios, the sheep that leaves his shepherd is easy prey for a wolf, a hyena, or any number of sheep-eating predators.

> *"Prone to wander, Lord I feel it, prone to leave the God I love."*

But this story from Turkey also illustrates the need for the shepherd to stay with the sheep. Maybe that is why Jesus said of himself, "I am the good shepherd. The good shepherd lays down his life for the sheep." (John 10:11)
Sheep need a faithful shepherd. We have one, the only one, in Jesus.

It was Jesus Christ, the Son of God, who was visited in Bethlehem by poor shepherds who had heard the news from angels of the Savior's birth. It was Jesus Christ, the Lamb of God, who gave up his own life on the cross in exchange for mine and for yours. It is Jesus Christ, the conquering King, who will return one day to separate the sheep from the goats, to gather those who have believed His word and had their sins washed away by His blood. This writer is one sheep who is keeping his eye, by God's grace, on the Shepherd.[10]

I would encourage pastors and elders reading this book that you are called by the Great Shepherd to love and tend the flock He has entrusted to you, which includes the good, the bad, and the wooly. And if you have been a pastor for more than two weeks (honeymoon period!), then you have seen all kinds. You have seen very few generals, to use Jeff's illustration, a legion of privates, and a disappointing number

[10] J. Mark Fox, *Family-Integrated Church,* (Xulon Press, 2006), pp. 89-91

of soldiers who have gone AWOL. The challenge is to learn to love each one where he is. Boys will be boys and sheep will be sheep. Boys desperately need a father who will love them all the way to manhood. Sheep desperately need shepherds who will love them all the way to the end.

I recently told my wife that my vocational ministry had risen to a completely new level. She knew what I was talking about and asked, "Did you have to help him go to the bathroom?"

There's a man in our church suffering from Parkinson's disease. When Ray first moved here and started going to Antioch, he was a retired accountant who had been successful in business following a time of service in the Army. His health was good and he and his wife delighted in spending time with their many grandchildren. They would take each one to places like Disneyworld, or to see his favorite team the Chicago Cubs play at Wrigley Field. Then a few years ago, Ray contracted this awful disease that has robbed him of the use of his legs, for the most part, and makes him dependent on others for the simplest of tasks. I went over to sit with him while his wife took their car to the shop, and I had the privilege of helping this dear man, my brother in Christ, go to the bathroom.

I have had many run-ins with the difficult sheep, the belligerent ones who seem to lie awake at night trying to figure out how to make life miserable for the pastor and elders. I confess that I have not always loved them well, but by God's grace, I am learning. But it is men like Ray who make ministry such a delight. Always grateful, always giving God glory, always encouraging others despite his own suffering, Ray is a sheep that makes me glad to be a shepherd.

May his flock increase.

Before we press on in the next chapter discussing some of the dangers in the ministry, let us spend a little time getting real with our Lord about our feelings. How do we really feel about the sheep under our care? Do we love them the way the Great Shepherd does? Would we die for them? If not physically, how about just laying down our schedule and frustrations for them? Do we have a pastor's heart regarding the flock under our care? Are we investing time getting to know the sheep? Consider this passage as we close:

> *Know well the condition of your flocks, and give attention to your herds. (Proverbs 27:23)*

Reflection Points:

1. Have I become discouraged in dealing with those sheep under my care?

2. Do I pray for those sheep that irritate me the most? Should I?

3. How am I doing on the five roles of a shepherd?

4. What would Jesus say to me if I met Him today about my shepherding?

5. Does my shepherding look like Jesus'?

Reflection Points: Those Who Support Them:

1. What type of sheep are you?

2. Are you easy to pastor or do you bite, nip, grumble, complain, and attack the shepherd?

3. How do you get along with the rest of the sheep? What would they say?

4. How do you become the type of sheep that is a blessing to lead?

7 The Dangers of Ministry

Put on the whole armor of God, that you may be able to stand against the schemes of the devil. (Ephesians 6:11)

Jeff

[11]The pastor looked ashen and near death when his friends carried him into our prayer room. I did not know him, but it was clear his time of departure was close. The dying man whispered into the ear of the senior pastor something those of us standing nearby could not hear. The two men locked gazes and then my pastor said, "I forgive you, and so does Jesus." The man on the stretcher began to weep. After they

[11] Some of the dangers addressed in this chapter have also been shared in Pastoral *Helmsmenship: The Pastor and Church Administration*. Since both books are attempting to help pastors, some overlap is helpful and inevitable.

left, my pastor shared what the man said. This pastor had committed adultery many years earlier in his career. Unable to find the strength to confess before, now as he faced death, he had to unload on someone. He had to find someone to forgive him. Bankers, lawyers, and construction workers can confess to adultery and keep their jobs. Pastors typically lose theirs. The burden of this unconfessed sin had been a yoke around his soul for decades and he needed release. I pray he found forgiveness before he met his Lord.

In chapter four, I mentioned the occupational hazards of the ministry - discouragement and disillusionment with people. Both of these will follow the pastor his entire ministerial life. They will ebb and flow like the tide, but make no mistake, they will never disappear. A carpenter can cut off a finger if he is not careful, no matter how skilled he may become. More than one master electrician has been killed by not paying attention, and many older pastors quit because they allow these two rascals, discouragement and disillusionment, to take them out emotionally.

Biographies of the prince of preachers, Charles Spurgeon reveal that he often had to be confined to his bed because of depression. Are you kidding me? Spurgeon? I read in one of those biographies that a main reason for the depression was that he did not feel like his life was making any difference. Oh come on, I have twenty of his books on my shelf! Not making a difference? No one, not even Spurgeon is immune to the dangers of ministry. Perhaps his emotional battle was chemical or even physically induced, but regardless of its source, many pastors struggle with being discouraged. In fact, read this verse carefully and notice Paul's transparency:

> *For we do not want you to be unaware, brothers, of the affliction we experienced in Asia. For we were so utterly burdened beyond our strength that we despaired of life itself.* (2 Corinthians 1:8)

Did Paul actually write, "Despaired of life itself" in that verse? No matter how you examine this verse, it seems that Paul was bummed out, and did not want to live any longer. Depression can do that to the strongest people, even godly heroes. Paul was overwhelmed, burdened beyond his strength, and wanted everything to end. Depression is a real danger to those in the ministry, and if you are struggling, please seek out help. Open up to someone. I know it is hard to be real and transparent with people when you are a pastor, but you must. Your struggle is not unique and there is help. For the sake of your family and your church, get it.

People can be downright ugly and mean sometimes. The emotional toll this puts on the pastor and his family by hateful Christian people is huge. Most pastors are godly people who love Jesus and are honestly attempting to help others do the same. The way these wonderful pastors are treated by other Christians however, would lead to you believe that these servants are the devil incarnate.

There is more to say about discouragement and we will in a later chapter. There are still a couple of other real zingers that we need to explore - immorality and cynicism. Both of these are running rampant among clergy and the devastation is huge. When a shepherd chooses to step into immorality, (notice I did not say fall) the sheep are often slaughtered. Moreover, when a shepherd becomes cynical, finding joy becomes difficult, his family suffers, and the pastor is tempted to become uncaring.

Immorality:

Almost from the very beginning of time immorality has been a major problem. Examples of multiple competing wives, sexual violence against women, incest, seduction, and prostitution can all be found in the Holy Bible. The book in the center of the Bible is a passionate love story, and Hosea was told to marry whom again? The wisest man of the Old Testament wrote several chapters about the consequences of moral failure, and he should know since he had 1,000 women in his harem.

"Men and women are different," scream the headlines, as if that is some new revelation. Ask any child over the age of five and he or she could tell the experts that much. Many pastors spend a significant amount of their time in marriage counseling, and a good deal of it ends up focusing on immoral behavior of some sort. Most pastors know that adultery, pornography, lust, and immorality of all kinds are rampant in the body of Christ. Given these facts, why do we act surprised that pastors commit sexual sin?

In my pastoral life, I have personally known multiple pastors who have given into temptation sexually, and read of even more via the information superhighway called the internet. Some have run off with another person's spouse and some have ruined their ministry through addictions to porn. The destruction caused by their moral failure is huge. Churches have closed their doors and new believers have walked away from Christianity. Marriages have been ripped in two, and young people have mocked Christ. Immorality is a huge danger to the pastor, and we are foolish if we do not take precautions against this scheme of our enemy.

So, what can we do about it? An excellent question and I have a few thoughts about it. First, as pastors, we need to understand that our enemy would love to destroy us. If we fall, not only do we do damage to our families and ourselves, but also all those that look to us will be shaken. Take out the head and the body will be killed. We have a bull's eye on our back, so we need to be on guard. We need to take precautions and we need accountability if we hope to finish strong.

Next, we need to set up clearly defined, unmovable boundaries or if you prefer, rules of engagement. I have several. I will not meet or be alone with a woman that is not my wife or daughter, never, nada, no way, not happening. I will refrain from frontal hugs and touching of other women — side hugs only and then just quickly. I do not need to feel her breasts against my chest and she does not need to feel my arms around her. Sorry, warning, mayday, mayday, flee from immorality! My passions are too strong, and who knows what the woman may be feeling? I would rather appear aloof and cold than to get into an immoral mess.

I do not counsel a woman alone. In over thirty years of counseling I have had only one woman become angry at me for not meeting alone with her; most thank me for it.

It is simply too easy for the protection aspect of men to kick in when a woman pours out her heart. I need someone else there, preferably my wife. Even better is to follow the Biblical guidelines explained here:

> *Older women likewise are to be reverent in behavior, not slanderers or slaves to much wine. They are to teach what is good, **and** so train the young women to love their husbands and children,*
> *(Titus 2:3-4)*

Men are attracted to women, and women are drawn to men. These are undeniable truths, and we ignore it at our own peril. Men and women, who are not married to each other, need to be very careful about spending large quantities of time together. Bonding can happen quickly and unbonding is difficult.

We are told by Paul to flee immorality (1 Corinthians 6:18) and I take him at his word. If I can avoid the temptation I am more likely to be successful than overcoming it in the heat of the moment. If we would avoid putting ourselves in those spots in the first place, we will have taken wise steps toward escaping moral failure.

With the proliferation of pornography, the battleground for moral failure has expanded. Every camera operator on every sports program on TV seems to find the cheerleaders, and just about any product sold needs a shapely young woman to sell it. Surfing the web without protection and purpose is an invitation to disaster. "Idle time is the devil's workshop" could not apply more than it does to the pastor who simply goes out to surf the web with no purpose. With one stray click of a mouse, total nudity can be found. Do we really need to go there? Will feasting on those images help our sermon preparation or ministry gifts? Will our sensitivity to the Spirit increase if we fill our minds with those pictures?

Men need to control what they look at and women need to cover up more. We need self-control and the fruit of the Spirit to reign in our lives. Immodesty and immorality are not fruits of the Spirit but lead to destructive deeds of the flesh. We are not to give the devil any place in our life and what we allow our eyes to feast upon is a big opportunity for our foe.

For some practical ideas, I would suggest making sure your computer screen is visible to anyone walking by the door. Just knowing that someone can come in and instantly observe what you are looking at will help provide some incentive to be more careful.

Make sure you have glass in your office door, or better yet, leave it open if you are counseling or talking with someone of the opposite sex.

Men also need to be careful with their flirtations just as the women need to be careful with how they dress. Most studies show that men are attracted by what they see, and women by what they hear and feel. As pastors, we are in a position of influence, and we must be careful what we say and do. God will hold us responsible for our actions and even our intentions so we must walk carefully in this arena. Those pastors that take advantage of the sheep sexually will pay a dear price.

For an exercise read Proverbs chapter 2, 5, 6, and 7 and notice the patterns, decisions, and consequences in the texts. Solomon explains in these chapters the dangers of seduction and moral failure. "So you will be delivered from the forbidden woman," "Her steps lead to hell," "Can a man carry fire in his chest and not be burned?" and "As an ox goes to the slaughter," paint a scary picture of the cost of moral failure.

If we as pastors give into moral failure, we will tarnish the Lord's reputation, crush our spouse, children and grandchildren, shake the faith of many of the sheep under our care, and give the enemies of Christ reason to blaspheme. The cost is high and there are no rewards worth this price tag. If you are already involved in an improper relationship, then leave it now. If you need help, get it today. Quit your church, break your computer, and move out of town if necessary. Whatever you need to do to get free is worth whatever the price tag is for that freedom. Do not be ignorant, you will be found out and the enemy will torment you until you repent. The only way out is confession and renouncement of the sin. Freedom can be gained by repenting and changing your behavior. If you are trapped, then run to the Lord and find release.

I have written a book entitled "*Courage to Flee*," that contains a great deal more practical help for battling this ministry hazard, so I will not share all of it here. The bottom line is that many pastors destroy their ministries, families, and future by not being on their guard against this foe of immorality. Please do whatever is necessary to avoid becoming the next statistic.

Cynicism

While there are many dangers we could develop for those serving in the ministry, I have chosen these two because they are so prevalent. Many pastors have given into sexual temptation and fallen, and probably even more have simply quit caring due to giving up because of frustration.

I know two good brothers who are slightly older than I am that are both resigning their church. While that in itself is not a big deal, for they are both in their sixties, what bothered me are the words they used in their announcement. Insightful phrases flowed out of them — "I am sick of pastoring," and "I am so glad to be away from all these people." I understand their thoughts for working with people can be a real pain; however, we must not end our ministries in a state of cynicism. Words like, "hate," "disgust," and "completely frustrated," often creep into the speech of the retiring pastor, and that is sad.

Pastoring involves working with people and as we all know, people are, well, people! The Scriptures use words like, "hard hearted, dull, stubborn, divisive, and unloving" to describe God's children. Often, pastors are on the receiving end of people's hurtful words and stubborn resistance. It is easy to become frustrated, and while some frustration is normal and even healthy, allowing it to move over into cynicism is not.

Cynicism is usually defined with words like, "mistrust," "jaded" and "scornful," and these typically refer to the motives of others. When a pastor slips into this mindset, he is on shaky ground. We are told by the Great Shepherd to love the sheep, lay down our lives for them, and serve them. We are not to hate them, mistrust them, or run away from them. People can, and often will hurt us, but we must watch our attitude and reactions to their actions. I am not discrediting or denying the temptation to become cynical, just reminding us that we must resist it.

The reality of the frustration of working with imperfect people will never leave. We are not perfect, and neither are those under our care. We are sometimes slow to change, and so are they. We resist the Lord's discipline, and so do others. We can be stubborn and unkind, and so can the sheep. Only Jesus is perfect and the rest of us are a work in progress. Sometimes it takes years for a truth to become part of our understanding and actually work its way into our daily lives. The same is true with those under our leadership.

Part of the reality of being in leadership is that we see something from God sooner and clearer than those that are following us. We will have a passion for a vision or truth that few others will. If it were the other way around, they would be the leaders and we would be following them. Since we may see a truth quickly, we are tempted to become frustrated with others who do not see it as soon or as clearly as we do. I believe that is why patience is both an attribute of love and a fruit of the Spirit. We must bear with one another in love.

The 8% Reality

Let me share a theory that I have that has helped me over the years in my battle against cynicism. This has nothing to do with the pain of rejection, betrayal, and heartache caused by people; I will cover that in a later chapter. This has to do with the visionary aspects that often lead to discouragement and becoming jaded towards those we are called to lovingly lead.

I call this theory "The 8% reality." We are all familiar with the parable of the sower and the seeds told in Matthew 13, and most pastors have probably taught on it a time or ten.

We also know that the point of a parable is typically singularly focused and contains one primary point for its interpretation. However, there are often many applications to the parables that we can glean, and this is one I use to help me deal with frustration. I hope it will help you as well.

We know that Jesus said that the sower sows the seed, and it lands on various types of soil. 75% of it produces nothing, and 25% finds good soil and produces a crop. Even within this 25% that produces, there is a difference ranging from 100% full production down to around 33%, or to use the Biblical terms, "some a hundredfold, some sixty, some thirty." What I glean from that is that even within the good soil there is a difference in fruit bearing. Great observation Jeff, so what does this have to do with fighting cynicism?

One cause of cynicism is the fact that we feel like we pour our hearts out, invest our time and emotional energy into people, and they just do not get it. No matter how clearly, passionately, or frequently we explain our vision; it is rejected or not completely implemented. Herein lays the point of my 8% theory.

The truth is that 75% will probably not ever get it. Even within the 25% that do buy into the vision there will be a variance to the degree of implementation. In fact, just about 8.33% will understand all of it. 75% of the seed produced nothing, and only 25% of the good soil produced a crop. (Disclaimer: I am not a math major so I round up or down as it is convenient for my story.)

The reality is that there will be a small percentage of people that buy into our vision completely, and these are represented by the 25% of seeds that land on the good soil. Within those that are attracted to our vision there will be a further division. Some people will understand it and walk out 1/3, and some 2/3, and a small group, say 8% will be completely on board with the vision. (Okay, I know that 25% divided by 3 is not exactly 8%, but see disclaimer above).

No matter how anointed we may be, regardless of how passionately we share our vision, there will always be a bunch of folks that simply do not get it, nor do they want it. God has assigned to each of us a realm of influence and that will be limited. Within this realm, there will be varying degrees of acceptance from those who follow us and to expect otherwise is a sure way to end up being cynical. One key to fighting cynicism is to make sure that we are investing in the 8% a significant amount of our time and emotional resources.

Sometimes it is easy to spend a vast amount of time in useless arenas. By that, I mean outside of our vision and gifting. For the record, no person is useless, and no one is outside of needing help and instruction, but part of what we need to learn is what *is* our arena and what is it that God has called us to do. Jesus taught the crowds but He primarily invested Himself in the twelve. Jesus also seemed to even narrow that down to the three closest to Him — James, Peter and John.

Let me end my thoughts on these dangers pastors face with a Scripture that has set me free:

> *O LORD, my heart is not proud, nor my eyes haughty; Nor do I involve myself in great matters, Or in things too difficult for me. (Psalm 131:1 NASB)*

God has not asked us to solve all the problems of the world or His Church. In fact, He said Jesus would build the Church, and I am quite sure He will do an excellent job. When someone asks me about a denomination or a controversial issue raging in the national spotlight, my response is Psalm 131:1. I can do nothing about it and no one involved is asking my opinion. I cannot carry the weight of it and I am not the one charged with fixing it. Jesus is and He will do just fine. My role is to pray for the matters before the One who can and will actually do something about them.

God has given each of us a realm of influence and He expects us to do the best job there that we can. My understanding of this reality is freeing. It releases us to stay focused on what our Lord has asked us to do for Him in building His Kingdom. Of course, we can see the problems, and we can pray, but worry, fear, doubt, and frustration over them is not an option. Jesus can and will make His Bride ready for His return. In the meantime, we are called to be faithful, diligent, watchful, expectant, and to invest in those who are following the vision God has given us. If we do these things for His glory, cynicism and immorality may knock on our heart's door, but we'll be simply too busy to answer it.

Mark

I wrote this column after one of our fall men's retreats a few years ago and wanted to share it here for your consideration.

A Man Needs His Brothers

I was at a men's retreat this past weekend with 40 of the men and young men of the church. At one point during the weekend, there were about 15 of us in the ocean, riding the waves, trying to avoid several Portuguese Man of War that were floating our way, laughing and enjoying the time together.

After a half hour or so, most left the water and ran off to do other things, and then there were just four of us dads left in the ocean. I cannot remember ever swimming at the beach when the water was like it was that day. The waves were coming fast and furious, each one bigger than any I could recall from past trips to the ocean. We hardly had time to get ready to float over one, or ride it in, before the next one came. When I caught a wave just right, it would take me speeding towards the beach. It was exhilarating. When I caught it too early or too late, it would spin me crazily around under water like a dishrag in the spin cycle.

It occurred to me later that evening as we were singing worship songs and I was preparing to teach, that I would not have been in the ocean that day by myself. It was just too risky. I was constantly checking on the other men to make sure they were still 'above their circumstances,' as I am sure they were doing the same for the others and me. We were staying close together, none drifting out further than the rest. We wanted to insure that the waves did not produce any casualties that day.

I remember the story from "The War" documentary by Ken Burns, about the US sailors who were in the ocean for days after their ship was destroyed by the Japanese. Sharks found the men and began to come, every day, to pick them apart. Imagine the horror of knowing that the sharks would be back in a few hours, and this time they may be coming for you.

The sad truth is that there are men in all of our churches who are facing the dangerous waves of financial destruction or marriage breakup or addiction to pornography or worse. The sharks of loneliness, depression, and despair are circling. Many of these men are isolated, drifting further from the shore, further from the brothers who are there and can help, further from hope. Some don't know where to turn because they have been consumed with pursuing their own dreams of financial success and relationships with friends simply have not been a priority. Others know exactly what to do and where to go, but their pride or shame or embarrassment keeps them drifting away while they look longingly at the band of brothers they used to know and love. The Bible states,

> **"A man who has friends must himself be friendly, but there is a friend who sticks closer than a brother."**

Men, we need brothers who will stick close to us, tell us the truth, and help us get past the breakers and into some calmer waters, men who will pray for us when we are in over our heads. These men will most likely not be found at the social club, the golf course, or the bar. Go to the closest church where the Bible is still being faithfully preached and men are still being challenged to be men...you will find some brothers there.

~~~~~

I would encourage every man reading this book, and especially pastors, to find a few brothers with whom you can
~~~~~

be completely transparent, at least once a week! I meet with four other men in my church every Tuesday morning at 6:30 at a local restaurant. We order and pick up our food, and then go to the same table every week, in a corner, away from the crowds. There we enjoy talking about the news of the day, family matters, work, and more while we eat breakfast. Then we get into the serious matter of making sure each of us is keeping his head above water. We ask about things like personal and family devotions, prayer with our wives, resisting sexual temptations, and other heart issues. These are men I trust, and I have shared struggles with them about a strain in my marriage or when I am having a particular issue with one of my children. After we have each shared an update and any prayer requests we have, then we take turns praying for one of the other brothers in the circle until everyone has been prayed for. I look forward to this meeting every week, and I know the other brothers do as well. It keeps us clean. You can hear a podcast I did with these men here, if you are interested in more information about how these groups work:

http://www.healthychurchradio.com/hcr022-iron-sharpens-iron-interview-with-four-brothers/

I also do something similar with the elders and deacons at Antioch when we meet together once a month. As we arrive at church on the first Sunday at 7:30am, we will pair off (with a different man each month) and go through a "Personal and Ministry Accountability" form with each other. I adapted it from one that John Piper has used with his leaders. You can find his form here:

http://cdn.desiringgod.org/pdf/pastors_accountability_form.pdf

It includes questions about our battles against ungodly thoughts, whether we have been with a woman in the past week in a way that could be viewed as compromising, questions about our financial integrity and even our eating and exercise habits. The purpose is to hold up a mirror once a month with the church elders and deacons to make sure that we are not disqualifying ourselves from leadership because of our own moral failures. It is a wonderful blessing to serve with men who take this seriously. We all know the truth of Paul's words, though, in 1 Corinthians 10:12, "Therefore let anyone who thinks that he stands take heed lest he fall."

Reflection Points:

1. Have I made myself vulnerable to the enemy in some way?

2. Am I walking in moral purity and in my dealings with those of the opposite gender?

3. Have I slipped over into cynicism somehow?

4. If someone followed me around all day and listened to my words, what would they reveal about my heart attitude?

Reflection Points: Those Who Support Them:

1. Are you in a dangerous relationship with someone who is not your spouse?

2. Are you willing to pray for your pastor so they do not fall into sexual immorality?

3. Will you seek to be a blessing to them to help offset those who are not?

4. Will you seek to be a person that that pastor can rely on, trust, and confide in without becoming judgmental?

8 The Blessings of Ministry

And when the chief Shepherd appears, you will receive the unfading crown of glory. (1 Peter 3:4)

Jeff

After exploring the dangers of the ministry, and before we delve into the emotional pitfalls inherent with our calling, it would be helpful to reflect on some of the wonderful blessings that go along with our life's work.

I am not sure what an unfading crown of glory Peter is referring to in the above verse, but it sounds great to me. It certainly does speak of reward, honor, acknowledgement, and the fact that it will not fade, meaning it will not need polishing or will not disappear. Who could ask for more?

Whatever is meant by this reward, we know that the Lord gives it to faithful shepherds and it will last forever. Nice.

I have met with hundreds of men over the years and almost all of them struggle with their chosen career path. The feeling of being inadequate in what they do, or the frustrations of believing they are not making any real difference in their world seems to be in everyone. When I share with them that this thought plagues most pastors, they ask, "How could you struggle, you are closer to God than I am?" What they are really saying is what most pastors know in our hearts — we should be close to God. We are expected to have an intimate relationship with our Creator for we speak for Him and about Him constantly.

In this expectation rests one of the primary blessings of our call — we are expected to have a close relationship with our Lord. If we are paid a salary of some sort, part of the reason for the payment is so we can be free to devote ourselves to prayer, reading of God's word and study. Now that is a blessing that many people do not have!

Most of us can remember the rather large Jewish character in Fiddler of the Roof belting out, "If I were a rich man." In the middle of Tevye singing and dancing around wishing he were rich, he utters a heart cry that should be ours — he wishes he could study the Holy Book for hours every day. One huge blessing we have in our calling is that we are to become experts in the Scriptures.

> *For the word of God is living and active, sharper than any two-edged sword, piercing to the division of soul and of spirit, of joints and of marrow, and discerning the thoughts and intentions of the heart. (Hebrews 4:12)*

If we become an expert in this living Word, we are indeed blessed! Pastors must become students of the Word of God and by doing so; our hearts will be in a much better place heart wise. Jeremiah told us that our hearts were desperately sick (Jeremiah 17:9) so any habit that helps to restore our heart to a healthy place is a tremendous blessing.

The temptation for pastors is to open the Bible only looking for sermon material, but we must resist this. We need to be refreshed, encouraged, and renewed in our thinking, as every other believer does. We have the joy of being free of other tasks so we can do just that — study the Word of God.

So far, we know that we will receive an eternal, unfading crown and by becoming well-trained students in God's Word, we have a renewed mind and clearer heart, but what other blessings follow our call? How about the realization that others are helped by our efforts? Regardless of how we may actually feel, people are helped by our teaching, praying, counseling, visiting, and leadership. We may not really feel that this is true, but it is. If we teach the Word of God, people will be helped. If we share the Word of God in counseling, they will be encouraged. Our prayers are effective because we are told they are in the Bible:

> *Therefore, confess your sins to one another, and pray for one another so that you may be healed. The effective prayer of a righteous man can accomplish much. (James 5:16 NASB)*

If we are saturated in the Word of God, then that which comes out of our mouth will produce good fruit. "Out of the abundance of the heart, the mouth speaks." (Matthew 15:18) and "A word fitly spoken is like apples of gold in a setting of silver." (Proverbs 25:11) People will be helped by just being around us if we are students of God's Word. Sharing the life-giving Word of God will help people in spite of our bumbling presentations. The life is in the Word, not in our delivery of it. I know we can hinder the impartation of the Word by our poor skills, but the point is, God promises that His Word will work His work. We can learn to rest in that truth while we sharpen our own skills in delivering it to those who listen to us.

There also is the salt and light factor, or as I like to call it, "The George Bailey Effect." One of my favorite movies of all time is, *It's a Wonderful Life*. This movie has kept me from leaving the ministry more times than I can remember. Most of you know the story — George is a banker that wanted to travel the world and do great things. Instead, he stayed in his little town and seemingly did nothing big. George was just a faithful husband, father, and all-around nice person. Maybe you feel that way as well. You had big dreams and all you ended up doing was pastoring a small church.

Disaster strikes George's world and in desperation he prays. While George is contemplating suicide, God answers his prayer and sends him a quirky apprentice angel named Clarence. I am not endorsing the theology here, just relaying the facts. Clarence comes up with a brilliant idea and gives George the gift of knowing what his world would have been without him. Don't we all wish we could see that reality at times? I wonder if we will in heaven.

George sees what his steady, plodding along, doing nothing life has accomplished by witnessing what his town and friends would be without his influence. The contrast is huge and I believe it is not just a Hollywood movie, but also a reality in each of our lives. We all are a George Bailey and we all make an impact on others; we just do not have a Clarence around to show us.

While I cannot prove it biblically, I firmly believe that in eternity we will worship and marvel at all that God did through the countless, seemingly insignificant actions of us all. Our lives matter and to a great many people; we just do not know it yet. We have the blessing of knowing that God uses us in the furtherance of His will in the lives of His children, and that is a blessing. Someday we will see fully what we only have a dim view of now.

Another blessing from our call is that we develop relationships, or at least we should. I know it can be difficult to maintain them, and sometimes it is extremely painful to continue in them, but all of us need others in our life. The very nature of our ministry requires interaction with people. We pray for them, counsel them, serve with them, correct them, learn from them, endure them, and sometimes we even enjoy them. In fact, John stated some harsh realities in his letters.

> *By this it is evident who are the children of God, and who are the children of the devil: whoever does not practice righteousness is not of God, nor is the one who does not love his brother. 1 John 3:10*
>
> *If anyone says, "I love God," and hates his brother, he is a liar; for he who does not love his brother whom he has seen cannot love God whom he has not seen. 1 (John 4:20)*

How we treat others is a good reflection of who our father is. John, the love apostle, gently states that if you say you love God, yet hate your brother, you are a liar.

Being in the ministry will put us in the middle of many relationships. We will have those that look to us for leadership and there will be others that we follow and learn from. Relationships are everywhere. There are relationships at home, work, play, and church. We cannot avoid relationships, so we had better learn how to walk in them. That is a blessing from God! By being forced to walk in relationships, we are guaranteed personal growth!

"Iron sharpens iron, and one man sharpens another." (Proverbs 27:17)

Because we must live with others in personal relationships, we will learn how to guard out tongue, control our temper, contain our flesh, and limit our freedoms. We must, for we are commanded to do all of those things by our Lord. People will help us grow and that is a blessing, even though sometimes it looks and feels otherwise.

Yes, there are challenges, dangers, frustrations, and heartaches in the ministry, but there are also wonderful blessings. We are promised a special crown from the Chief Shepherd. We are required to spend time in study and prayer, which leads to personal growth and a healthy heart. We are used by Our Father to further the work of Jesus' kingdom on earth, which should strongly encourage us. We are required to develop relationships with God's other children and the growth potential from these is way beyond our ability to grasp.

There are many other blessings, but the ones just mentioned are sufficient to encourage us to continue on in our service in the Body of Christ. We are blessed beyond what we deserve by the One who called us into this glorious ministry, and for that, we should be extremely grateful.

Mark

I love Jeff's illustration from *It's a Wonderful Life*, and I believe there is a "George Bailey Effect" for each one of us. The problem is, with many pastors, is that we have very selective memories. I tend to remember with excruciating detail every negative comment about me, my preaching, my ministry, or just about anything else that I can take personally. Then I forget the words of gratitude that have been spoken over the years by members of the church genuinely thankful for my ministry.

Years ago I started an "Encouragement File" and started putting letters and cards I received from people in the church or community who wrote to me to thank me for something. As the years went by and we all forgot how the mail system works, I started printing out encouraging e-mails, texts, or tweets and putting those in the file folder. Now it is so large that I need to go through it and weed it out some. But I don't. Neither do I go through it and READ the notes and letters. In fact, I bet in 27 years of pastoring the same church, that I have looked through that file less than 5 times.

Whenever I do, I am reminded of a ministry I had with a family as I walked them through the death of a child. Or the times I counseled a young couple as they prepared to start a life together. Or the number of people who have read my newspaper column and written to tell me that it helped them or even changed the direction of their life.

I just recently got a phone call from a man who said in 2008 he was at a crossroads with his career and he felt like the Lord was calling him to do something completely different. He had been rescued from drug and alcohol addiction as a young man and had his life turned around through a relationship with Jesus. And in 2008, he was feeling a tug on his heart to do something intentional to help other young men who were just as he used to be. But it would mean quitting his job, moving his family to Florida to become part of a ministry there, in order to learn how to do the same thing here in North Carolina. He didn't know what to do, and was really wrestling with the decision. Then he read one of my Saturday columns, entitled "Pray the Lord Will Eject More Laborers." The column came after a mission trip to Ghana and I wrote: "Jesus says to would-be followers: 'Go your way.' You know what 'go' means in the Greek? It means, *Don't stay*. Isn't that fascinating? After Jesus was raised from the dead, he said to his followers, 'As the Father has sent me, I also send you.' As he was about to ascend into heaven, he said it again, commanding his followers to go into all the world and make disciples. Do you see? This whole 'I want you to go' theme tends to emerge."

The man told me, "Mark, that column changed my life. And the direction of it." Now he has a very successful ministry to men who want to be free from addiction (*Living Free Ministries*), and I praise God that He would stoop to use one of my little 600-word newspaper columns to help direct one of His sons.

I heard a pastor say a long time ago, "God can hit a straight lick with a crooked stick." It's true of every one of us pastors. We are all crooked sticks, but the fruit of our ministry is a product of God's power working through us in spite of our weaknesses. One of the greatest blessings of my ministry has been maturing (finally!) enough to understand that what Paul said, "When I am weak, then I am strong" is true. (2 Corinthians 12:10b) I am so weak. My tongue can be so sharp. My thoughts can be so fleshly. My heart can be so deceitful. But praise God, His strength is unlimited. His Words are life. His thoughts are infinitely wise. His heart is perfect.

With all the challenges and heartaches that walk along with me as a pastor, I would not trade this life for anything.

In the next chapter, we will explore some of the emotions that all pastors deal with, and how to handle them in a righteous way. Before we move into this revealing chapter, let us stop a minute and reflect on the many blessings we have in the ministry.

Reflection Points:

1. Have you thanked God for the many blessings you have by being a pastor?

2. Can you think of other blessings that were not named in this chapter?

3. If you could change just one thing about pastoring, what would it be, and why?

Reflection Points: Those Who Support Them:

1. Have you encouraged your pastors this week by sharing with them what they mean to you?

2. If the pastor receives a reward for their service to Christ, don't you think those that help them will also share in it?

3. What could you do this week to let your pastor know how much they mean to you and what their investment in your life has meant?

9 The Emotions of Ministry

Jesus washed Judas' feet and I don't think I could have done that without biting them.

Jeff

A very dear pastor friend of mine shared with me recently a hurtful phone call he had received. Some long-term members of his church had moved out of state and called him asking if he would give them back their entire tithe. A little taken back, my friend asked them why they wanted it. Before I give you their answer, let us fill in a bit of history.

These long-term members had sat under this delightful brother's teaching, prayer covering, counseling, and leadership for years. Weddings, funerals, evangelism events, missions' outreaches, hospital visitation, and jail ministry, just to name a few pastoral type activities my brother performed, were all observed by these folks. In other words, they could be just like someone sitting in your pews right now.

I am not calling into question the motives of these people, just their insensitivity. Studies show that pastors are often underpaid, under loved, criticized intensely, expected to be perfect, attend every event or meeting, know everybody's name, including children, their birthday and anniversary, not to mention where they work and their schedules. They are expected to hit a home run with every message with each one being better than the last one. They are supposed to be always smiling, never grouchy, never out of the Spirit, but overflowing with grace and producing lush, abundant fruit. I will resist going into family expectations right now because we will address some of that pressure in the next chapter. In short, pastors are supposed to be exactly like Jesus, but not divine. No pressure huh?

The reason these dear saints wanted their tithe back was because now they were going to a church where *real* ministry was actually taking place. Their words were something like, "We are finally attending a church where they are actually doing something." Nice. Please send us our money back because these people are doing something for Jesus, unlike you mister. Not their exact words, but certainly, what was communicated. Even though he was smiling, the pain in my brother's eyes is understandable and all too common among pastors.

People can be brutal and not even know they have just crushed the pastor. Sometimes the comments are humorous like, "Wow, great message today, pastor, not like your normal ones." Or, "The Spirit really spoke today, what did you do differently?" All too often pastors hear, "I am just not being fed here anymore," or, "I don't know what's wrong, but there is no life (joy, love, or whatever) here." Do people think that the pastor decided to kill the Spirit or to share a miserable message from the pulpit on purpose? Who is responsible to eat again? You can lead a sheep to pasture but you cannot make them eat...or was that a horse? How old are you when you begin to feed yourself anyway? By the way, if you are only eating one time a week, you are starving to death spiritually.

Someone has rightly stated that a pastor needs to possess a heart the size of Texas and the skin of a Rhino. I fail on both counts.

Many pastors have heard personal, hurtful comments about their ministry. It would be one thing if such accusations were coming from the outside, but many of these type comments are spoken from people that we attempted to love and serve. We expect to be attacked for our faith but we are not always prepared for the assaults that come from those we love. It has been observed by animal experts that sheep lack sufficient teeth to do damage to other animals, I would beg to differ. I know many pastors who have been mauled nearly to death by attack sheep, and it is not a pretty sight.

Most pastors love Jesus and the people that are under their care. I know hundreds of pastors and not one of them is in the ministry for power, money, or to control people. Each of them answered God's call to come and die for those that the Lord would place in their sheepfold.

The point of bringing this up is not to evaluate whether the comments are valid, but to give a glimpse into the pain that many pastors carry. The purpose is not to whine or complain about the sufferings endured by the pastor. Every job has its drawbacks, and since the ministry is focused heavily on people, relationship issues will be involved. Because people can and do hurt one another with their words, pastors are often primary targets for someone's harshness.

Of course, pastors fail those under our care, for only Jesus is perfect. Yes, there are times when we are harsh, insensitive, or uncaring. There are pastors that are very strong in their views and unwilling to yield. Pastors are human and are not Jesus. We are not divine and we fail. Given that truth, the point is that pastors are often accused falsely, assigned horrible motives, and not given the same grace that the accusers expect or demand, and this can leave deep scars.

Burnout is a term used in the business world and also used in reference to pastors. Most of the time this happens not from the workload, but from the people drain. Studying, praying, relationship building does not usually destroy a pastor; personal attacks do. Emotional wear and tear is what causes most pastors to leave the ministry and go into selling insurance or out onto the speaker's circuit.

Most of us can handle having an action questioned or corrected; questioning motives is another story. If someone confronts a pastor and tells them that what they said was harsh, that is one thing; telling them that they were harsh because they are a mean person takes it to a new level.

Proverbs correctly states:

> *Death and life are in the power of the tongue, and those who love it will eat its fruits. (Proverbs 18:2)*

It is important that we speak words of life one to another. What we sow we will reap. We can disagree agreeably and we can speak the truth to one another in love. Life and death are no small matters.

Preaching Pressure

I mentioned in an earlier chapter about the teaching and preaching load on the pastor and let me expand this just a little bit more here. Consider these verses:

> *Not many of you should become teachers, my brothers, for you know that we who teach will be judged with greater strictness. (James 3:1)*

> *Be diligent to present yourself approved to God as a workman who does not need to be ashamed, accurately handling the word of truth.*
> *(2 Timothy 2:15 NASB)*

Most pastors take their teaching and preaching seriously and so we should. We are told by James that we will incur a strict judgment based on what we share from God's Word. Jesus was very harsh with the Pharisees and one reason was they distorted the Word of God. We need to be careful what we speak for we will give an account to the Lord for our words. If we mislead God's children, we will be in trouble with their Father.

Beyond the fear of judgment, there are the expectations placed on pastors by the listeners and by the pastor themselves. We who speak on a weekly basis want to do an excellent job of presenting the truth we have learned to those who listen to us. We study, pray, take notes, read study helps, learn languages, practice, use audio and video tools, and listen to others teach, all with the express purpose of helping those listening to us to grow in their walk with God.

Who wants to fail in the pulpit? Who works all week long to present a miserable, boring message? Most pastors care deeply about presenting a message that is helpful to their listeners. Some speakers are more naturally gifted than others are. Some pastors are excellent storytellers and some have marvelous drama or creative skills. Some do not. Most of us are just trying to do the best job we can with the gifts we have.

The pressure to perform is huge. The desire to be effective and communicate clearly is our goal. Who wants to strike out? Everyone wants to hit a home run. Every time. Each message should be perfect. Each sermon should be well illustrated, insightful, engaging, thought provoking, entertaining, yet deep, and chocked full of God-given, ready to implement tools to succeed. Every time we stand up, we should hit it further than the time before. No pressure. Add in the super star preachers on the radio and TV that our listeners rave about, and most of us sink in the mire of discouragement.

The reality is that not every message will be better than the one before. In fact, the comparison is unfair to begin with. Each gathering is a unique, not to be repeated event. The Holy Spirit has specific goals for each gathering and no two meetings will ever be the same. Nor should they. Our goal as pastors needs to be to consistently and faithfully present the Word of God, while accurately handing the Scripture. We need to pray, study, and to the best of our abilities, present the Scripture to the people. The harsh reality is that even the very gifted preachers still hear the same complaints of their listeners — "I'm not being fed"; "The anointing seems to have lifted," etc.

Leading singing and preaching is a weekly, and sometimes multiple-times-weekly event. No one and I mean no one, hits a home run every time up at bat. Most home run heroes also lead in another category of stats — strikeouts! Having an expectation to hit a home run every time we bat is the same as believing that every message will always be better.

Each message stands alone and we who give them must leave the results in the Lord's hand. Have we been faithful to pray and prepare? Are we doing everything we know how to do to improve? Are we staying close to the Scripture? If we can answer yes, then we are doing well.

Splinter Theology

Another significant emotional struggle pastors deal with is betrayal. Since most pastors love deeply, the possibility for relational pain is high. Loving and entering into other's lives opens the door for vulnerability. Many pastors, and to an even greater degree their spouses, have been hurt deeply by friends who walked away.

People change churches every day of the week and often they walk away with little or no explanation as to why. Pastors, who have invested a significant amount of emotional energy into the relationship, are left feeling hurt, betrayed, and sometimes confused. Churches that have some sort of follow up with those that leave will sometimes find out the reason for the departure. Other times the reason for leaving the church comes through the grapevine. Whatever the reason given, the pastor usually feels it personally.

I was an associate pastor for eleven years and people leaving the church never really bothered me that much. I would see the tears in the senior pastor's eyes, but mine were dry. Then I became a senior pastor and more understanding came into my life. Just about every person that leaves our ministry causes hurt in one way or another. The only ones that don't cause hurt are the folks that leave due to moving or someone that had no personal connection to the pastor.

Many people leave due to some dissatisfaction, complaint, need not being met, disappointment, offense, not fitting in, can't find a place to serve, not being fed anymore, don't feel loved, feeling judged, overlooked, not part of the "in group," children don't like it, no joy there anymore, and the list can go on for several more pages. All of these can, and often will be taken personally by the pastor. Most folks that leave a church do not tell the pastor why, but will many times tell others. It will eventually get back to the pastor and the discouragement is huge.

To explain the pain and distraction a bit more let me delve into my "Splinter Theory." You may not be familiar with this term but I know you can relate. In the midst of a family leaving the church under painful conditions, people will attempt to encourage me by saying, "It is only one family, and there are many more here that love you. Why is this bothering you so much?" Enter Splinter Theory.

When someone has a splinter in his or her finger or foot for example, it really is a small thing. In fact, that splinter when looked at in reference to the entire human body is almost negligible. The rest of their body is doing well, yet where is the pain and how much attention do we give to this small matter? When there is a splinter in our finger, even though the rest of our body is happy, we focus on the pain. Until we deal with that tiny speck of wood or metal, our time, energy, and emotions are focused on it.

When someone leaves our ministry in a painful fashion, regardless of how everyone else may be doing in the group, our focus naturally turns towards the pain. Instead of chiding the pastor for not appreciating those that have stayed, pray for them to refocus and recover from the wound quickly. Giving a hug and nod of understanding will probably help more than telling them what they already know. Just a thought the next time you see that look in your pastor's face. The pain is real, even if it is only small by comparison.

Many pastors state that these type events are behind their own marriage struggles and personal failures. Spouses often take up the pastor's offense and sometimes this leads to bitterness and unforgiveness. Relationships are strained and a cloud can hover over the entire ministry due to the pain. Assigning wicked motives to the pastor who invested above and beyond what their scheduled allowed often produces despair on his part.

Please be careful what you say and share with others, for it will eventually get back to the pastor. If you have a problem with the pastor, go to him personally and do not make a bad situation worse by sinning with gossip. The pain and division is horrible, and in most cases, could have been avoided.

How to Leave a Church

A friend shared a teaching CD with me a few years ago. The pastor speaking was British and he had been pastoring a church for over 26 years. This engaging speaker was addressing a pastor's conference with about 1,000 in attendance and he said the following: "I am going to share with you the sum total of what I have learned over all these years of pastoring. Ready?

People come and people go.

This dynamic teacher slowly said, "They leave Jack Hayford, Charles Stanley, and all big name preachers, they will leave you. They left Jesus, they will leave you." His point was clear, get used to it for it is unavoidable.

Now, that is not all he shared but it is enough to reinforce what I know to be true. People come and go for a variety of reasons and no one is immune. This speaker shared the same reasons people left his church that almost every pastor has heard — no love, not being fed, do not fit in, church didn't do enough, anointing has left, etc.

People leaving are fairly common, and so is the pain from their actions. Many times it happens that someone leaves a church, and then later on, the person feels like they have to justify the action to those that want to know why. Instead of just leaving peacefully, justifications need to be given. Sometimes these reasons are real and sometimes they are not. Sometimes the reasons end up being a personal assault on the pastor and these hurt the most. Please be careful as to what you share and why you are sharing it, for it will eventually get back to the pastor. If you would not say it to the pastor's face then please be careful of what you say about them when they are not around.

I believe there are only a few reasons for leaving a church: First, if there is unrepentant sin/heresy involved in the leadership, then leaving is the best option. Second, if the vision of the church is not in line with what God has told you to do, then leaving may be a better option than staying and being frustrated. All of us change and grow and sometimes our vision changes as well. Third, as I mentioned earlier, if you are involved in an immoral relationship with someone in the church, then flee. Of course, there are other potential reasons, but many of the ones typically given are simply excuses and fail to deal with the real underlying issues.

If you believe God is leading you to leave a church then may I suggest the following to limit the pain to the pastor and the rest of the Body of Christ? Your pastor has probably been a sounding board to you for many issues - marriage, counseling, job situations, child raising problem, and many other spiritual questions. You have built some sort of relationship with him and sought his advice on many topics and now that you are making a huge decision, shouldn't it be natural to talk to him about it *before* you make it?

How much better would it be for you to go to your pastor when you first begin to think about leaving and ask them to pray with you, and for you. You may be thinking, my pastor would never counsel me to leave their church so why bother to ask them their opinion. Perhaps, but on the other hand, if God is leading you wouldn't you want the blessing of those in leadership on your move? Cannot the Sovereign God of the Universe speak to your pastor in order to confirm what you believe He is saying to you? If God were indeed leading you, why wouldn't you want confirmation? How much better to leave with a blessing and the confirmation of leadership, than with a broken relationship.

Your pastor loves you and cares for you more than building his own church and if God is leading you to leave, most pastors will attempt to confirm that for and with you. There have been many times when someone came to me, we prayed, and it was clear that his or her time was finished at my church. God had something else for them to do and that is what I wanted them to do. You might be surprised at what your pastor would say after praying about this move. At least the pastor would know what you are thinking, and the reasons behind your praying, and that in itself, would limit the pain in your leaving.

Pastoring is an emotionally intensive lifestyle. Hurts and wounds are part of life and the pastor's world is not immune. I have pulled back the veil just a little bit to give you some insight into how some of us struggle. My goal was to urge you to pray for and to stand with your pastor. If you are a struggling pastor then I trust that this chapter has at least let you know that you are not alone or abnormal. Every pastor has his battlegrounds emotionally and we need people around us to help.

Pastors Leaving Their Church:

My friend Michelle asked me a question that is worth discussing here. Michelle is a professional counselor and has encountered many broken pastors and their families.

> *I spend time in my office with the pastors who experience difficulties/temptations/divorce... and especially helping the spouses of the Pastor who has been disciplined for moral failures, or ousted from the church entirely. I work with the families who lose their church family, support system, and identities because the Pastor loses his job. What happens to the families of the pastors who are ousted?*□

The next chapter will deal with the family in greater detail, but please do not read over Michelle's question too quickly. What happens to the *family* when a pastor leaves the church? When a pastor fails, what does the family go through? In our thirty years of ministering, we have walked through many dark days. "Wc" is thc corrcct pronoun because the family walks right beside the pastor. Most of the assaults, abuse, insults, rejections, and accusations have been directed to or about me, but my wife and children have also endured them. Most of us know that taking up someone else's offense is easy and harder to deal with than the person who was offended in the first place.

When a pastor leaves a church, turmoil can potentially reign in his home. Friends and relationships are often broken. Many times a move is involved, and we all know how much children love moving away from their friends. If the removal was because of sin, the spouse bears the shame right alongside the guilty pastor. If the removal came from a power struggle lost, the family is tempted to become bitter.

The broken pastor not only has to deal with the church but attempt to bring healing to their family. It is not easy. Most occupations do not have to deal with this dark side of ministry. When I left a corporate job, my family was not attacked verbally nor carries any shame. I wish the same could be said from leaving a pastorate.

Every pastor invests part of his soul into the church they are serving. So does the family. When the break comes, so does pain. Even when a pastor leaves of his own free will, pain still follows. Moving and changing churches is part of the lifestyle of a pastor. Pain will always be there for those that care.

Even in the situations where a pastor must be removed due to some sort of moral or ethical failure, there is a way to help the family. Those charged with the removal need to be careful to limit the damage if possible, as in only sharing what is absolutely necessary, and with those that need to know. Follow up phone calls, emails and concern will help ease the pain. The worst thing to be done is simply to forget or ignore them. Out of sight out of mind may be true, but it hurts those who seem forgotten. I know it is hard to know what to say, but saying nothing is worse. Always err on the side of mercy, grace, and encouragement and much pain could be avoided.

In addition, many children grow bitter by watching their parent be attacked, abused, not supported, underpaid, mistreated, removed and then neglected by those that were served. May we never add to their perception that Christ is like that, for He is not.

Mark

Here's one of the reasons I don't stand at the back as people leave the sanctuary after a service. People say awkward things to you about your sermon! One pastor said he has had people say things like this to him: "You always manage to find something to fill up the time." Or: "I don't care what they say, I like your sermons." Or: "If I'd known you were going to be good today I'd have brought a neighbor." Or: "Did you know there are 243 panes of glass in the windows?" Or: "We shouldn't make you preach so often."

All kidding aside, the Bible makes it clear that those who labor to serve the church in leadership should be honored, not ridiculed. Paul said,

> **"Let the elders (or pastors) who rule well be considered worthy of double honor, especially those who labor in preaching and teaching." (1 Timothy 5:17)**

The word for labor is kopiao, which means, "to work to the point of fatigue or exhaustion." Let's face it. There is a perception among some in our culture that it is only those who work with their hands at manual labor who toil. But that's not God's perspective, and it certainly wasn't Paul's, who spoke of the toil of the minister with the same word with which he spoke of the toil of the hard working farmer in 2 Timothy 2. Paul said in 1 Corinthians 15:10 that he worked harder than all the apostles did, and the word he used for "work" is kopiao. And in Galatians 4:11, he uses the same word again: "I am afraid I may have labored over you in vain." Same word again in Philippians 2:16, "holding fast to the word of life, so that in the day of Christ I may be proud that I did not run in vain or labor in vain." This responsibility of laboring in the word and in doctrine and in caring for the spiritual life of the church is WORK. There is physical and mental toil in the work of the elder.

Are there men in the ministry who have given the rest of us a bad name because they do NOT work hard or because they are otherwise not qualified to lead a congregation? Yes. Those men are not really biblical pastors or elders. There are men like that in every area of life, slackers who do just enough to get by or even less. But slack dentists should not make us disrespect excellent dentists. In fact, it should make us all the more grateful that there is a dentist we can go to who takes his job very seriously and who works hard to be excellent in his field.

In addition, Alistair Begg makes a point that is worthy of repeating here, that those who study to become a lawyer have to work hard and prepare to pass the bar, and then it's over. Those who have a CPA have to work hard to prepare to pass the exam, and then it's over. You pass the examination and then you do your work. Elders and pastors do their work, and then they have to face their examinations. You work all of your life and then you are examined, and on that day you will discover whether your work, your labor, was wood, hay and stubble, or silver, and gold, and precious stones!

What if you are unhappy with your pastor now, and don't want to wait to see what happens to him in the hereafter. You could try this: A Lutheran newsletter has some tongue-in-cheek suggestions for church members unhappy with their pastor: "Simply send a copy of this letter to six other churches who are tired of their ministers. Then bundle up your pastor and send him to the church at the top of the list. Add your name to the bottom of the list. In one week, you will receive 16,436 ministers, and one of them should be a dandy. Have faith in this letter. One man broke the chain and got his old minister back.[12]"

---

[12] https://bible.org/illustration/chainletter

Or, you could follow the Bible. John MacArthur writes,

> "There are always people eager to falsely accuse a man of God. They may do so because they resent his calling, reject his teaching, resist biblical authority, resent virtue, or are jealous of the Lord's blessing on his life."[13]

I thought about the dunking booths at the fair. The pastor and elders are the ones in the dunking booth, most often. They are easy targets, and in some churches, it is almost considered a sport to see how quickly the pastor can be discredited so the church members don't have to listen to him or follow his counsel. But how does the church protect the elders from such foolishness?

Go back to 1 Timothy 5:19.

> **"Do not admit a charge against an elder (or pastor) except on the evidence of two or three witnesses."**

Witnesses. Plural. "Admit" is from a Greek word that means, "receive, welcome, entertain in your mind, consider." In other words, we are not even to listen to an accusation of a pastor or an elder.

It takes two to gossip: one talks and the other listens. But what if you refuse to listen? Then you don't enter into sin yourself and you put a stop to the mouths of those who would accuse the brethren. "Faithful are the wounds of a friend." If you are a friend to that one who wants to attack

---

[13] John MacArthur, *The MacArthur New Testament Commentary, 1 Timothy,*(Moody Press, 1995) p. 221

the pastor, then you will be willing to speak the truth in love to them.

I remember when a family left the church in anger several years ago that some of the talk going around was an accusation against the pastor and the elders that was based on misinformation given out by the angry family. One of the men told me he sat down with his teenage son and told him what had really taken place. He said, "After my son heard the truth, he was sad that he had believed a lie about the pastor and the elders, and he became an even greater advocate for them in prayer and in encouragement about them to others."

Amen. May many more like this young man be raised up in our churches.

As pastors, God has given us a family, and much of our primary support will come from them. Before we delve deeper into those relationships and unique struggles, let us stop a few minutes and spend some time thinking and musing before the Throne of Mercy.

Reflection Points:

1. Why do you think God gave us emotions? Did He make a mistake?

2. As a pastor, have you given into despair, discouragement, or bitterness?

3. As a pastor, have you placed too much emphasis on people's comments about your sermons?

4. Have you allowed bitterness or unforgiveness to have a place in your life due to the hurts received from pastoring?

Reflection Points: Those Who Support Them:

1. Have you ever thought of your pastor's struggle with people leaving before?

2. What could you do to help the pastor deal with the pain they so often carry?

3. What could you say to your pastor to help them with the preaching pressure they carry?

4. If you are considering leaving your current church, will you do so differently now?

10 The Family Circle

The view from a fishbowl is beautiful says the non-fish.

Jeff

Unlike[14] most career choices, the family is intimately involved in the ministry. They have no choice. Even if your spouse and children do not want to be, they are. From being considered a non-paid staff person to being expected to maintain a pristine, perfect life style, the family is impacted by the pastor's profession.

It is typically not stated, but the pastor's spouse is considered part of the package when the pastor is hired. Counseling duties, administrative and organization supervisor, perhaps de facto decorator and chief bottle washer, the spouse is expected to be involved. So are the children. If they can play the piano and run the nursery, even better — all of course at no pay.

[14] Some of this chapter is shared also in *Pastoral Helmsmanship*

Beyond the expected, unstated workload of the family members of the pastor, is the pressure put on the family to live up to unrealistic standards. Since pastors are expected to be super spiritual saints, the family must be equally strong. The pastor and their spouse must never quarrel and the children must be shining examples of near-perfection.

My children would often hear comments like, "You watch *that* movie and you are a pastor's kid?" The movie in question was "Angel and the Bad Man" with John Wayne, but it really would not matter what the movie was. The expectation is that the pastor and his family just sit around singing hymns and praying all day. The pastor's family is viewed many times under a microscope, and sometimes it gets annoying under that glare.

What would be considered completely out of line in the business world seems to be just perfectly fine in the Church. In my years working for corporate America no one ever attacked or criticized my family. I wish that could be said for the House of God. Like any other person, it really is hard to remain in a sanctified condition when someone is saying mean things about your spouse or child. At times, I would like to do unto others what they are doing unto my family, but that is another story, and not very Christlike.

We can, however, do a few things if we are under this pressure regarding our spouse and children. First, be upfront during the hiring process or whenever beginning a new pastorate. Explain what your spouse and children will and will not do. If they want to be involved, great! If not, that should be equally fine. If it is not fine, then further discussion should be held up front, not as you are leaving in hurt and anger. Second, deal with offenses as they arise and do not just stuff them. It is very easy for your spouse or children to slip into bitterness. We must teach them how to forgive, how to confront, and how to walk on in grace. This will need to take place early and often in the ministry.

The Scripture tells us to "Know well the condition of our flock," and that includes the one under our own roof. We must allow time for venting, discussing, and open, honest communication to take place. We must foster an environment where we can freely share what is going on in our own hearts. Spouses and children will hear details of people's lives that are not common knowledge and they will need help in learning how to process it all, not to mention the fine art of confidentiality. There is a burden in ministry of knowing details of people's lives that few others know. Our family must be trained on how to deal with this knowledge.

PK Jokes and Family Problems:

Sadly, many "PK" jokes are true. Children of the pastor are sometimes ignored and offered on the altar of ministry, and this becomes obvious by how they behave, or probably better stated, misbehave. Ministry can become addicting and wise pastors will not allow it to take over their life. God gave the pastor a family and He expects it to be taken care of. The pastor's family is a part of the church and should be entitled to equal time. In fact, I would make the argument that if we fail here, what we have done elsewhere will not offset it. Consider these passages about the qualifications for an elder/overseer/pastor for a moment before we move on: (Emphasis added is mine)

> *The saying is trustworthy: If anyone aspires to the office of overseer, he desires a noble task. Therefore an overseer must be above reproach, the husband of one wife, sober-minded, self-controlled, respectable, hospitable, able to*

> *teach, not a drunkard, not violent but gentle, not quarrelsome, not a lover of money.* ***He must manage his own household well, with all dignity keeping his children submissive, for if someone does not know how to manage his own household, how will he care for God's church?*** *He must not be a recent convert, or he may become puffed up with conceit and fall into the condemnation of the devil. Moreover, he must be well thought of by outsiders, so that he may not fall into disgrace, into a snare of the devil.*
> *(1 Timothy 3:1-7)*

> ***If anyone is above reproach, the husband of one wife, and his children are believers and not open to the charge of debauchery or insubordination. For an overseer, as God's steward, must be above reproach.*** *He must not be arrogant or quick-tempered or a drunkard or violent or greedy for gain, but hospitable, a lover of good, self-controlled, upright, holy, and disciplined. He must hold firm to the trustworthy word as taught, so that he may be able to give instruction in sound doctrine and also to rebuke those who contradict it. (Titus 1:6-9)*

It is interesting to me that of the many qualifications required for leadership the primary one expounded upon is family related. It is as if God knew that a pastor whose family was out of order could not keep the church in an orderly fashion either (sarcasm intended.) While the pressure to be perfect from others is over the top, the requirement from God to be in order is not. A pastor whose home is not functioning is not able to stand with complete authority and ask that his followers should have their home in order. Those that live with us will reflect what they are seeing and learning in the home. We will teach as much by what we model as what we say.

Lest we become overly discouraged with these verses, a process is implied and not perfection. "Manage his own household" does not mean there are never any problems, it means that the pastor is aware of them and doing everything within his power to deal with them. There are no perfect parents, only a perfect Heavenly Father. If memory serves me well, He also had some disciplinary issues with His first two children. We will always have relational issues to deal with, we just need to make sure we take care of them before they get out of control and cause damage to the Church.

The home is a wonderful testing and proving ground for servant leadership. Marriage and child training will give us insights on how to help others in these arenas.

I did an informal survey one time in some of my social media world asking pastors what percentage of their time was spent in marriage/family counseling. The results were about expected — the vast majority of it. As pastors, we are leaders and leaders walk ahead. Our families provide a wonderful training experience for us to learn how to help those following us. Wouldn't it be a great goal to have all those PK jokes turned into wonderful examples to follow instead of being a source of mocking?

Rejection

In the previous chapter, the emotions of the pastor were briefly explored. The spouse and children also play a part in this emotional battle. The spouse sometimes takes up the offense that the pastor just chooses to let go. So do the children. Many pastor's spouses and children become hard and bitter because of how badly their spouse or parent was treated. I know several middle aged people that hate the Church of Jesus Christ today because of how their father was treated as a pastor when they were younger. That is not the only reason, but it is a primary one. They grew up in a home where their father was verbally abused by the leaders of the church they were attempting to serve and their venom still flows out freely today. Yes, they need to forgive and move on, but the Church also needs to do a better job protecting the pastor and their family.

In the typical church, rejection will come from just about every angle. Lifelong friends can become offended, find themselves on different sides of an argument, and leave the church in an instant. Relationships can break and never be repaired.

The friends that leave the church also leave the family relationships and the damage to the spouse and children can linger for decades. The result is future friendships can be hindered due to fear of more rejection. The more broken relationships, the greater cumulative impact on the family.

It is very important for the pastor and his family to develop relationships that last. Even if they have to find some outside of where they serve, relationship stability is critical to the well being of the family. The sad truth is that sometimes relationships are difficult to have inside of the church. Illusions and false expectations are placed on the pastor and his family and when they are not lived up to, relationships tend to break. It is hard to have transparent relationships with those under your care.

Rejection is part of ministry and it will never be removed entirely so the pastor has to be aware of the price being paid by their family. Open lines of communication between the spouse and children must be constantly checked and reinforced. Every broken relationship the pastor endures is also felt in some degree by the family. God gives grace and by that grace, we survive and heal. As pastors, we need to make sure that the grace we received is shared with our family members.

There are many lessons to learn through hurt and rejection. Our Lord was rejected and despised, so we share in His pain. Our hearts can become tenderer to others if we guard against bitterness and cynicism. Empathy can grow in our hearts after we walk through the pain of rejection and betrayal. When someone is sitting across from us in deep pain, we are not quite so quick to dismiss it or to give some religious cliché after we have suffered. We can learn to cry with those that cry because we have tasted the pain ourselves.

Scriptures that gives me great comfort and often explains the unexplainable is found here:

> *Blessed be the God and Father of our Lord Jesus Christ, the Father of mercies and God of all comfort, who comforts us in all our affliction, so that we may be able to comfort those who are in any affliction, with the comfort with which we ourselves are comforted by God. (2 Corinthians 1:3-4)*

Many times I have no answer as to why something horrible happens. Divorce, death, disease, and all manner of heartaches afflict the followers of Jesus. After hearing of the pain and crying together, I will usually quote theses verses. I do not understand all of what is going on, but I do know that God will make use of everything, including our pain. One usage is to prepare us to help others.

We walk through rejection and pain and we draw near to God for comfort. Sooner than later someone will come to us who has a similar pain, and then we can share with him or her how we got through our heartache. God is like that. A wise pastor will instruct his family on how to walk through pain, rejection, and heartache with an eye to being able to help others in the future. Nothing is wasted in the Kingdom of God, not even our hurt and rejection.

Even though many will come and go, the pastor can find staunch allies and support from the family that he loves and values more than the ministry. We are first believers in Jesus, then a spouse, parent, or grandparent, before we are a pastor. We would be wise to remember such things with how we spend the bulk of our time. Most pastors would never counsel their members to ignore or deprive their family for their career, so why would we model such things?

It is easy to become hard, bitter and to raise a wall of protection around our emotions due to hurt and rejection. We must learn how to forgive those who wound us, and to help our families do the same. Forgiveness is a choice we make because we are forgiven. We did not deserve forgiveness and perhaps those that hurt us do not either. But, we must forgive them.

People change over time. We have, and so will those that hurt us. We must not "freeze frame" someone in time. We relive a hurt, an event, a betrayal over and over and reopen the pain of the wound each time we do so. The temptation is to lock someone into that period of time and assume that they have not grown or changed. If they are a believer in Jesus, we can rest in the fact that God will change them. None of us are the same people we were five, ten or fifteen years ago. Chances are very high that neither is the one that hurt you. We must not lock them into that image, but allow for the truth that we are all growing and changing. Forgiveness is like that.

Mark

I am so thankful that Jeff included this chapter in the book. Living in the fish bowl can be excruciating to a pastor's family. Barnabas Piper just completed a book entitled *The Pastor's Kid*. He writes,

> "So many PKs carry so much pain and anger and sorrow with them. Some of them have fallen into bitterness, and others are rightly doing the hard work of trust in Jesus to help them through."[15]

Pastor's Kids and Pressure

I had the opportunity on a recent family vacation to talk to my children, and my daughter-in-law Kari, about what was hard for them growing up as pastors' kids.

Kari: "For me it was probably just the pressure....there was a lot of pressure just to be good because if we weren't, it would discredit Dad. That definitely was a big motivator, aside from Christ motivating us to stay on the straight and narrow...you know, I can't rebel, because Dad would lose his job!"

Micah: "I was going to say the same thing. Not only feeling like we *had* to do things right, but because people expected us to do things right. That was the hardest part, what I perceived other people expected. It was always a relief when someone would say, 'We don't expect you guys to act any different than any of the rest of the kids in the church!' I also remember the jokes among the kids when *their* dads became

[15] Barnabas Piper, *The Pastor's Kid* (David C. Cook, 2014), p.11

elders at the church, we would say, 'Welcome to the limelight! Welcome to the perfect world!' ☺

Susanna: One thing that was 'hardish' was that everybody in the church seems to know everything about you, everything you do, so you can't be private.

Caleb: There were things I kept from dad because I was a pastor's kid...maybe being a PK at times kept me from being honest.

Jesse: "I never felt any pressure. Maybe it was because I was the model child." (laughter)

Kari: It was harder in our family because our standards were a lot more conservative than the rest of the church, so we stood out. That added to the pressure, because we thought, 'We have to turn out OK to prove that our standards work."

Question: What about being a PK was a good experience? Made you thankful that you grew up that way.

Jesse: "It gave me more opportunities to help with things in the church."

Micah: "Because most men don't get paid to study the Word, and you were, that helped..., you had the vision, and you set the example in spiritual things, having family devotions, and other things that were positive for us. We definitely benefitted from your depth in the Word."

The pain and bitterness in the pastor's children and sometimes in his wife can come from so many different directions, as Jeff pointed out so clearly. There are pitfalls in the ministry, and no guarantees that our children will make it safely through childhood as healthy, Christ-loving adults. But I believe with all my heart that there are a few things we pastors can and must do to give our kids a fighting chance.

First, develop a relationship with each of your children. Don't sacrifice them on the altar of ministry and expect that will be OK with God. "Hey, Lord, I am going to take care of everybody ELSE in this church and I expect You to take care of my *kids*. Right, Lord?" No. I often tell pastors, "The credibility of your ministry stretches not one inch further than your front door. Be a faithful husband and father first." The relationship we pastors have with our children is crucial and the key to holding onto their hearts. I love the quote by anonymous: "The bridge of relationship must be strong enough to carry the truth across." That brings me to a second point.

Second, don't be a hypocrite. This is often why the bridge collapses and 'truth' can't crawl across if its life depended on it. Pastor's children who see that he is a phony, that he is a totally different man in the pulpit than the one who lives in their house, will reject him and worse, they may reject the God he claims to know. So, be the same man at home. Humble yourself when you blow it and ask forgiveness of your son or daughter (or wife) quickly.

Third, enjoy your children. Be their dad. Take an interest in the things that interests them and spend time with them just having fun. Whenever my children talk about their favorite memories from their childhood, they talk about family vacations, or playing whiffle ball in the back yard, or just sitting round the table laughing and talking. We have fun together and I love being with them.

Again, there are no guarantees. But I can tell you from first-hand experience that pastors' kids don't have to be the rebels in the church. They don't have to be the first to leave the faith when their group reaches adulthood.

I wrote a newspaper column several years ago about this, entitled "A Glad Father Enjoys the Fruits of His Labor."

Last week I had the opportunity to spend the better part of an afternoon with a good friend of mine. I was flying to Kenya and had a six-hour layover in Detroit. So, my friend came and picked me up at the airport. We found a little cafe close by, and had a pleasant lunch together. Then we asked directions to the nearest Starbucks, and spent another two hours there, enjoying the fact that neither one of us had to be anywhere that afternoon, there was nothing pressing us, and we could simply enjoy the company, the wonderful smell of coffee brewing, and the laughter of good friends.

We talked easily of old times, swapped stories, joked around, and just enjoyed being together. I reflected later on the plane how much I love this friend of mine, and look forward to the next time we can be together. The funny thing is, though we have known each other for 21 years, our relationship has changed drastically in the last two.

You see, this friend is also my oldest son. Micah attends college about an hour from Detroit, and was able to come down and hang out with Dad for half a day. We talked about the courses he is taking in college and the things he is learning about life. We discussed the job offer he has waiting for him after he graduates this May. We laughed about college pranks, and we agonized together about the Panther's loss to Seattle. We talked about theology and about career choices and about marriage.

When Micah dropped me off at the airport and we hugged, it felt as natural and as easy to say, "I love you" to my son as anything I have ever done.

What a blessing! I felt like I was sitting down to a banquet of fresh fruits and vegetables that my wife and I had planted in a different season. All of the agony of backbreaking toil in the hot sun was forgotten because the harvest was in, and the feast was prepared. The labor was eclipsed by the sweet reward. The fruit was delicious and satisfying.

I am not writing this to point to myself as a good father. Believe me when I say that I have made as many mistakes as anyone. I remember a basketball game that almost came to blows because of my own pride and stubborn competitiveness. Micah's cooler head prevailed, and we were spared what could have been a devastating blow to our relationship. I remember many times when I disciplined in anger. I remember several years of awkward embarrassment between us as he grew into manhood and the hugs were fewer than they should have been, the expressions of love forced at times, absent at others. I remember the times I didn't do the thing my son needed, and the times I did or said the wrong thing. But I am eternally grateful, and I give praise to the One who is able to take my meager efforts and my mistakes and redeem them for His own glorious purposes. He has certainly done that in my relationship with Micah. And I trust God will do the same with each of my children.

The Bible says, "A wise son makes a glad father, but a foolish son is a sorrow to his mother" (Proverbs 10:1). This is one glad father.

Before moving on to the next chapter, why not take a few moments and reflect. Ask the Lord if there is anything He wants to say about the flock under your own roof.

Reflection Points:

1. As a pastor, am I protecting my family enough while we serve in the ministry?

2. Am I aware of the struggles that my spouse and children may be having with rejection?

3. Am I addicted to ministry and modeling an imbalanced life to those I serve?

4. Is there anyone that I need to forgive or set free from the freeze frame of bitterness that I keep them in?

5. Have I discussed this with my spouse and children to see how they are doing with anger or bitterness?

Reflection Points: Those Who Support Them:

1. Have I ever said anything nasty or hurtful about the pastor's spouse or family?

2. What could I do to protect the family of my pastor from pain and heartache?

3. Have I been faithful in praying for my pastor and his family?

4. Do I need to go and ask for forgiveness in this arena?

11 We Still Need A Barnabas

And though a man might prevail against one who is alone, two will withstand him—a threefold cord is not quickly broken. Ecclesiastes 4:12

Jeff

While we must take a stand-alone sometimes, being by ourselves in ministry is a death wish. We all need others in our life to assist us, comfort us, support us, chide us, and love us. If you are reading this chapter, you have probably gained some insights into the struggles that most pastors face. I hope your prayers for them will increase and that you will be motivated to help ease the burden they carry. Even the strongest leader needs support. Moses needed Aaron and Hur, David had his mighty men, Jesus had the twelve, and Paul had Timothy, Titus, and Barnabas. We all need others to help us, and I pray you would want to be that person.

I want to share with you a brief section from another book that I penned entitled, *The Master's Handiwork.* In a section of that book, I was discussing the people that have made a significant impact into my life. These men serve as my Barnabas and I want to give you a glimpse into what they mean to me. After reading this, I hope you will be challenged to become one to your pastor.

*One of my favorite characters in the Scriptures is Barnabas. This guy takes Saul the church persecutor under his wing when no one else would, defends a young disciple Mark from some harsh accusations, and is known as the *Son of Encouragement*. How could you not love a guy known by that name? Being a pastor is sometimes a very lonely, discouraging life. It has been the guys fulfilling the role of Barnabas that have often kept me going when I wanted to quit. What a source of strength and encouragement it is to have men who love you, care about how you are doing personally, support you, and pray for you.

I have men that meet often just to pray for my family and me. Can you imagine how that makes me feel? These guys, all employed family men, take time out of their life to lift me up to the throne of Grace. I am truly humbled and deeply honored by their sacrifice. As one friend of mine likes to say, "You have to be careful what you say around these guys because they will do it." I feel like King David when he longed for a drink of water from a certain well. Three of his mighty men heard the request, made the trek, fought through the enemy, and brought back the drink. David appreciated the sacrifice and poured out the drink as an offering to his Lord because he knew he was unworthy. So do I.

These men have their problems, and none has been perfect men, but since when did that become a prerequisite for love and service? There have been family issues, financial struggles, sin problems and just about everything that anyone else deals with daily, yet they continue to be Barnabas to me. I can call any one of these men and they will give me time, support, a listening ear, their opinion and prayer. While each is different in personality, all are men of God that I depend on for support. There was no way Moses could hold his arms up without Aaron and Hur, and there is no way I can be an effective pastor without these men.

As I think about these men, I am challenged to be like them. Will I drop what I am doing for others that have a need? Will I pray for other people that are hurting and need support? Do people have to be careful around me with what they say or I might just do it? May I grow to this place. Every pastor needs strong, servant-oriented people who are holding up his arms, will you be one? Everyone can pray, serve, and be a support to those around them. I can attest to the fact that there is a dynamic that takes place when the pastor is being supported in prayer, and when he is not. Prayer does change things; someday we will know how much.*

Loneliness

I just stated that being a pastor is sometimes a very lonely job. Be there for your pastor. Reach out to the pastor by letting him know you are praying for him. If he can, and if it is something he desires, spend time with him, and just listen. Most of the time pastors are the dumping ground for everyone's problems, but whom do they talk to when it is time to offload their burdens? When someone walks up to the pastor and says, "Can I talk to you for a minute," it usually means at least two things: it will be bad and it will not take a minute.

It has been hard over the years to be open with others. There have been times that I ventured into dropping my guard a bit and it simply blew up in my face. Pastors struggle with anger, emotions, and wounds and sometimes they need a safe place to share. Will you be that place? I shared once with a group of my leaders a letter I *wanted* to write. I did not intend to send it, but boy, did I wish I could. One leader was very offended that a pastor would even think such things! What he did not know is that was about my tenth draft, and it had mellowed quite a bit. The leader left my church shortly after I opened up my heart just a little. It was years before I would risk going there again and being transparent with my emotional struggles.

Try an experiment one Sunday. Walk up to your pastor and say something like, "Pastor, I just wanted to share with you how much I love Jesus, my spouse, my family, my job and how blessed I am to be part of this wonderful church." As the pastor stands there speechless, just hug him and walk away smiling. Or if you prefer, take a picture of him with his mouth hanging open and send it to him for a laugh.

Another thing your pastor needs is your honesty. As you build a relationship with him, give him honest feedback. Flattery is not needed and is not helpful. If you are going to say something about the sermon for example, be specific. Instead of saying, "That was great today." say, "The point you made about grace today really spoke to me in my situation at work." The first one sounds like something that has to be said out of being polite while the second sentence has greater meaning.

Tangible Gratitude

I am a blessed pastor. The men around me look for ways to show me they appreciate me, including financially. I have to resist them because they are too generous. I know, you may not have that problem and it might even make you angry that I do, but I cannot help that. God has surrounded me with generous leadership, and I am blessed.

If you are part of the leadership, and are involved in setting a pay package for your pastor, please be generous. Pastors work long, hard, emotionally draining hours. They are on call 24/7 and most of them give way beyond what is required. Their families carry a burden and expectations that almost no one else does. Most pastors are highly educated and whatever you pay them, it will not be that much per hour. I know there can be abuse and I am not talking about that here. Many pastors are simply underpaid by church boards that are sometimes selfish or naive. Wow, that sounded harsh. Really? How about considering what the Scripture states:

> *Let the elders who rule well be considered worthy of double honor, especially those who labor in preaching and teaching. For the Scripture says, "You shall not muzzle an ox when it treads out the grain," and, "The laborer deserves his wages." (1Timothy 5:17-18.)*

How about this concept. Let the board that makes these decisions find the average salary of its members and then double it for the pastor. I can hear the snorts right now from that concept, but is it really out of line? I am not suggesting that this should necessarily be the process, but how do you go about setting the pastor's salary then? The old, all too familiar sentiment is, "Lord, You keep the pastor humble, and we will keep em poor." Is that really godly? Would those making the decisions about the pastor's pay package really want to live with it? If not, then why not?

There are many tools available to find an appropriate pay package for the pastor. Stop by the National Association of Church Business Administrators website and order a copy of their annual salary compensation book, for starters. My point is not to dictate how you set your pastor's salary, but to have you consider if you are properly communicating to your pastor their value and your love. Most pastors do not serve for the money, but how they are treated will help determine their joy in doing so.

Little gestures can mean so much. Appreciation cards, bonuses, notes expressing gratitude for the pastor's service: all of these help replenish his emotional bank account. Vacation time, comp days, and guarding the pastor's schedule are something the leaders around them should encourage and enforce. Pastors need to know their efforts are appreciated, just like everyone else. Volunteers need appreciation for their service and so do the pastor and his family. Invest wisely with the small details here and you will reap the reward of a contented pastor.

Mark

Paul speaks to the heart of the pastor who is lonely, discouraged, feeling like giving up in 2 Corinthians 4. I love this chapter, and you will notice as you read it that the Apostle with a pastor's heart says twice, "We do not lose heart." When we pastors are afflicted, perplexed, persecuted, we do not lose heart because we are *not* crushed, we are *not* driven to despair, and we are *not* forsaken.

Howard Thompson, my mentor and friend, told me he knew a pastor in Oklahoma who was also a licensed pilot. "Every Monday morning my friend would get in his little Piper Cub and fly out over the city to quiet his thoughts and to shake off the discouragement that most pastors feel every

Monday. When he would get over the heart of his city, he would lean his head out the window of the plane...and spit." Hey, whatever gets you from one Sunday to the next, right? But we pastors need to remember, and those who are in our churches need to know, that we are called to a ministry of suffering.

You may minister to a family, pouring your heart and soul into them for five years, and then one day you wake up and hear that they have left the church and taken five other families with them and they are starting a new church across town. You feel like you have been struck down.

You may be standing in a home where the husband has been missing for two days, and you have stopped by to let the wife and her children know that you are praying, when there is a knock on the door and two police officers say with sad faces that they have found her husband. He is dead in a hotel room, and he has taken his own life. You are perplexed.

You may be on your way to the hospital where a family in the church has been living for months because their 15 year old son has leukemia, and you have visited many times and talked and prayed and read Scripture with this godly young man who loves the Lord but is losing the battle to cancer, and on your way this time you get the phone call: he is gone. Their fifteen-year-old son will never get to grow up, have a wife and children, and serve the Lord. You are hard pressed with grief.

You may be counseling a man not to walk away from his marriage and counseling his wife not to give up on her husband, only to find out that they are both involved in adulterous affairs. Then you hear that her mother and her sister are angry with the pastor and the elders, even though we did all we could to help this marriage. That is persecution.

Look again at 2 Corinthians 4. You may be hard pressed, or perplexed, or persecuted, or even struck down. But the emphasis is on the NOTS.

- You are NOT crushed.
- You are NOT in despair.
- You are NOT forsaken.
- You are NOT destroyed.

Praise God! Ours is a ministry of suffering, and it is what we are called to. But listen, pastor. Some of the greatest power of your ministry will not be what the people see in you when things are going well, but what they see in you when you are struck down. When you are perplexed and in despair and persecuted and in the midst of it all, you are praising God and manifesting the truth of God's word. That's when they see that the excellence of the power is not in you but in GOD! That may be when they REALLY learn that He who raised up the Lord Jesus will also raise us up with Jesus. Listen, pastors, we have to learn how to suffer well. Do we know how to suffer well? Even when our suffering seems to make no sense at all? As Spurgeon said, we must learn that though we may not be able to trace His hand, we can trust His heart. Every suffering we endure for the sake of Jesus and His church has a divine purpose. Do not lose heart.

Before we move into sharing a few practical ideas regarding ministry, why not stop and prayerfully reflect on what has been shared?

Reflection Points:

1. As a pastor, am I afraid of being honest with those that surround me?

2. If I have been burned in the past by being open, will I move to a place of trying again?

3. Is there anyone, anywhere whom I can trust and open up to?

4. Do I have any friends?

5. Am I grateful for the financial provision God has provided?

Reflection Points: Those Who Support Them:

1. Have I judged my pastor?

2. Am I willing to reach out to my pastor and love him in tangible ways?

3. If I am part of the compensation process, is my heart for blessing the pastor?

4. What one thing could I do this week to encourage my pastor?

12 Practical Pastoral Tidbits

Reinventing the wheel is a waste of time, and if I did it, it would most likely be square.

Jeff

Since the Book of Acts, there have been church leaders. Pastors, elders, shepherds, bishops, or whatever else they may be called, they are there, and their writings abound. One goal and joy we as pastors gain is to glean the truth presented in their books, sermons, and notes. With the advent of the internet, we can access the writings of many of the greatest leaders in church history. I provide a listing of some excellent resource sites in the back of this book and the best thing about them, is they are all free.

We can learn from the best minds in history. C. S. Lewis, Francis Shaffer, Augustine, Spurgeon, Morgan, and a host of gifted leaders have left us a legacy. Part of our study time should be invested in reading the thoughts and sermons of the leaders of the past. I marvel at the depth of insight and vocabulary used by these dear saints. At times, I think it would be better for my church if I simply stood up and read their anointed words instead of my own. I have not yet, but still might.

In addition to the mighty men of old, there are great study tools available from the leaders of today. Blogs, discussion groups, and the entire social media realm provide an endless opportunity for learning and networking. There is no reason for a pastor to be alone or uneducated in our day. While we may argue over the damaged caused by the invention of technology, the opportunities they provide for growth is not debatable.

Along this line of thinking, most of us do not work alone. Even solo pastors of very small churches have fellow leaders around them, and we must learn how to work together to further the work of the Kingdom if we want to multiple our impact.

Your Leadership Team

Regardless of your church government setup or size, your church will have leaders. These people may be titled or not, but everyone knows who they are. Pastors can be intimidated by them or collaborate with them. I would strongly recommend the latter choice. If we give up caring about who gets the credit, we will accomplish a great deal more for Jesus' kingdom. If we focus on what we do well, and release others to do what they do better than we do, everyone wins.

Some pastors are afraid of losing their position if another leader excels. While this may be a real fear in a few churches, it should not be the norm. We encourage the brothers in our church to take turns teaching on Wednesday evenings. I pray that each of them would become a far better teacher than I am. What a blessing to have strong men that can teach! Their families will be better off and so will the church. What exactly is wrong with having multiple, gifted people in our churches? What will suffer from having those that excel do what they do best instead of the pastor just scrapping by in mediocrity?

If your gathering is blessed with multiple gifted people, that reflects well on your leadership as the pastor. Leaders produce leaders. Gifted leaders recognize and release others into their calling. Leaders do not do everything, but they focus on what they do well. Wise leaders learn to surround themselves with others who can do what they cannot or should not do. How is that a bad thing again? Surrounding yourself with gifted people is a sign of wisdom, not foolishness.

If you read in the Old Testament about some of the accomplishments of David's mighty men, you might be astonished. These guys were one rugged bunch. I bet David couldn't do what they could or did. Yet, like all wise leaders, David attached himself to the best he could find. So should we. David did not have to go into a pit on a snowy day and kill a lion, but he had a friend that did. How about taking on hundreds or thousands of the enemy? David surrounded himself with an elite group of men and as they excelled, he rose with them. We should not be intimated with talented, gifted people; we should embrace them and thank God for them.

If you are one of those talented people, your goal is simple — support the leader. Listen with the ear of a servant and anticipate what the leader needs. Be the man or woman that the leader can depend on. If you say you are going to do something, then do it. If you look for ways to serve, you will be amazed at what you find. God gave you gifts and talents, and He expects you to use them for His glory. Every leader needs help and support, and the one called alongside to help is just as important and needed as the leader.

As pastors, we sometimes inherit leaders that we do not want. The Kingdom of God is primarily relational, so we must learn how to get along with God's other children. Every family has its moments when the father has to intervene and bring correction to misbehaving children, and the Church family is not very much different. A wise leader will learn how to appeal to those who are older, encourage his peers and lead those who are younger. God is quite capable of bringing correction, and I wonder how many church splits could be avoided if the leaders simply prayed, instead of attacking one another.

There are of course times when action is required, but even in these times, the relationship should be primary. Ego, pride, my way or the highway thinking, has little to do with servant leadership and everything to do with death being unleashed in the Church. If we esteem everyone as better than ourselves, and if we follow Jesus' Golden Rule, much strife and conflict could be avoided.

What do we do as leaders when there must be change? Pray, seek the Lord; allow God time to change hearts. Avoid reacting and demanding our way. Seek input and counsel. Words spoken can never be taken back. On many occasions in my case, it would have been far better to be quiet than to speak. We must value relationships over petty issues. Yes, there are issues worth fighting for, and even dividing over, but how many church splits happen over trivial matters, hurt feelings, or because of a harsh word spoken carelessly?

If we were going to make big changes, I would recommend going slowly. Ninety-degree turns often lead to multiple relational wrecks, whereas five-degree turns allow for smooth acceptance. Yes, there is a place for decisive leadership. There are times when being strong is the correct answer. I just wonder how often those attributes are used as an excuse for not waiting and growing in patience.

I served on an elder board that had a wide range of ages, from mid-twenties to a brother that was in his early eighties. As the many weighty issues of a large, growing church were brought before us, the reactions of the men were insightful. The young men typically wanted action and they wanted it now. Excited, often dramatic phrases and emotions were used to explain why something must be done, and yesterday would have been better. After everyone had their say, the oldest elder would raise his hand and begin, "Now brothers, God has not changed and He is not in a hurry. We need to pray, seek His face, and allow time for His will to become clearer." This wise saint would say more, but usually not much more. Peace would engulf the room, and we would not react, but seek the will of the Lord. Old age does that. Less reaction and more pro-action come from age and experience.

We need to make sure we surround ourselves with older leaders if possible, and learn to listen to them. Yes, we need youthful zeal. We need the energy of the young, but we must have the balance of the elderly and wise. Our churches will be as stable as the leadership. Choose wisely.

Networking

Every pastor needs friends and other pastors for fellowship. So do their spouses. I mentioned that sometimes it is hard for a pastor or his spouse to be completely open with those they lead. We still must have someone that we can share with and trust, and who will understand us without judging. Pastoring is a unique life, and only those that have lived it, understand it. Those on the outside can see some of the issues, but actually living it allows for mutual depth of understanding.

I have watched several army movies, but I have never spent the night in a foxhole alongside another man. Those who have tell of a bonding that we can observe, but still not fully understand unless we experienced it. The same is true in just about any situation. Experiencing the same lifestyle gives insights into a reality that those outside of it can never fully grasp. Pastors need other pastors. Pastor's wives need other pastor's wives.

There are many groups available to assist this need. Again, through technology it really does not matter where you live, you can find others if you really want to. I belong to several pastor groups. Some are local; some are located thousands of miles from me. I receive life and help from both. Google+ Hangouts, video conferencing and chat forums all can shrink the distance. If we look, we will find fellowship and partners in the ministry. Check out the resources in the back of this book if you cannot find anything local.

It is also very helpful and refreshing to visit other churches. Step out and see what others are doing. Without too much effort, we slip into a routine. We can deceive ourselves into thinking that we know everything there is to know. Every time I have ventured into another church service, I have walked away with something of value. Perhaps it was a new way of doing something or maybe it was a reinforcement of why we do not do what they did that way, but it is always helpful.

Weddings and funerals also provide an excellent learning tool for pastors. I enjoy listening to others as they lead and often will make notes to make sure I do not lose what I learned. No two pastors or churches are exactly alike and if we maintain a humble attitude, we can learn from any experience. After all, our main job is to pastor those under our care, and if we learn a new or better way of doing that, that is excellent. No one is beyond learning and growing if we remain open and humble.

Revelation

When using this word, I am not referring to the book but to insight. In my early days of pastoring, the man I learned under stated something one day that changed my life. In addition to his helpful chiding to always use the same size paper to write my sermons on, he stated, "There is not an absence of revelation, but a lack of capturing it."

Almost everyone can relate to driving down the road and having a great thought. "Wow, I need to write that one down," goes the thinking. Then the phone rings, or something catches our attention on the radio or we arrive at where we going. What happened to the great thought? Later on when I try to think about it, I draw a blank. Bummer, I had such great plans for that thought, but it is gone. It may reappear or it may not, most times, it does not.

I have learned over the years to write it down, speak into a recorder, bark into my smart phone, or do whatever is necessary to capture it. If I wait, I lose it. The older I become, the quicker I lose it, if I do not write it down. Many nights, as I lie there trying to go to sleep, thoughts come into my head. If they are great thoughts, I have been known to jump out of bed, find a pen and paper, and write them down. Why? I do not want to lose them and they will fly away if I do not capture them. How about you?

Focusing on what Matters Most

The old story is told of the farmer that began his day with the intention of plowing the south forty. As he was heading towards the tractor, he noticed the front porch step was broken. On the way to get the hammer and board he saw the gate needed to be fixed so it hung squarely. While working on the gate the observant farmer saw how untidy the tool shed was. Then he saw a hole in the fence, the horses needed brushing and the barn door needed painting. As the farmer went through his day, he accomplished many tasks. The south forty however, was never plowed.

Pastors, like the farmer above, are always faced with too many tasks for the hours allotted. If we lose sight of what is important we will end up busy but not necessarily accomplishing what really is critical. We can watch our marriage and family slide away. Our prayer and study times drift into quick snippets of rushed grasping for something clever to say on Sunday, instead of seeking the Lord for His direction and purpose. The tyranny of the urgent is always with us. We must learn to prioritize and choose wisely with the time we have.

I began this book talking about vision and how freeing it is to have one. We must not lose sight of what God called us to accomplish through busyness. Time management is really a misnomer for we all have the same amount of time available to us. What we need is schedule management.

I use the ABC system, but it really does not matter which one you use, just use one. The ABC system entails two five to ten minute blocks of time at the beginning and ending of each workday. At the start of a day, I list out everything that I have to do that day. It does not matter how long the list, just write it all down. After you write it down, then go back and place a letter by each task. A's should be the most important;

"I have to get this done type tasks." B's are important but not critical. C's are those tasks that I would like to finish or do but they really are not that important. I know what you are thinking; all of my tasks are A's. Trust me, they are not.

As you place the letters by the tasks, a picture should come into focus. Decide to work on the A's as much as you can. Most of us typically work on the C's because they tend to be quicker and easier. We swap short-term gratification for investing in what matters the most.

As you prepare to end your workday, take out your list again and review it. Scratch off what is finished and reprioritize what is left to do. Life happens and interruptions are a part of life. Very few of us will have a finished list at the end of our day. After you go through your list, lay it down and walk away. Congratulations! Tomorrow is almost planned for you. When you hit the job in the morning, take out the list, and begin to work on the A's. Rinse and repeat.

This system has worked for me. It may not for you, but what do you have to lose by trying something different? Maybe the south forty will actually be plowed if we have a list.

We as pastors must also learn to delegate and empower others. Andy Stanley shared in his book, *Next Generation Leader*, the concept of focusing on our strengths. As I read this book, the truth of what was being shared hit me. There are those that love to do what I hate doing. Someone may actually enjoy the tasks that I dread. In fact, they will not only enjoy it, but also do a much better job than I ever could. Why should I struggle and hope to achieve being mediocre when there is probably someone out there that would excel? We must be willing to let go and empower others to assist us.

If we will focus on what God has gifted us to do, and if we will walk in the vision we have, we will accomplish more for the Kingdom. We will be able to invest our limited time in what we are good at and leave the other tasks to those that do them better.

I have a friend of mine that said something like this to me one day as he was observing my feeble attempt at mudding sheetrock: "Jeff, why don't you go study or read a book and I will attempt to fix what you have done here." My buddy was an excellent carpenter and could do almost anything as a handyman. I on other hand am very good at demolition, but not so much on fixing or building anything. While I could have continued to throw mud on the wall, the end result would not be anything near what my friend would produce. My pride could be hurt or I could realize that he was correct. I went and read an excellent book that proved to be mutually satisfactory to all involved.

Mark

Reproduction

John Maxwell wrote, "We teach what we know; we reproduce what we are."[16] That means pastors need to invest in the people around us who have the leadership ability to carry on the work that is bigger than all of us. The last night of Martin Luther King's life, he gave a speech in Memphis, TN that is eerily prophetic. He said,

> "I don't know what will happen to me now. We've got some difficult days ahead. But it doesn't matter to me now. Because I've been to the mountaintop. I won't mind. Like anybody else, I would like to live a long life. Longevity has its place. But I'm not concerned

[16] John Maxwell, *The 21 Irrefutable Laws of Leadership*, (Thomas Nelson, 1998), p. 148

> about that now. I just want to do God's will. And He's allowed me to go up to the mountain. And I've looked over and I've seen the Promised Land. I may not get there with you, but I want you to know tonight that we, as a people, will get to the Promised Land. So I'm happy tonight...I'm not fearing any man. 'Mine eyes have seen the glory of the coming of the Lord.'"

The next day, King was struck down by an assassin's bullet. He paid the ultimate sacrifice. But his leadership had inspired others who took up the mantle and carried on with the cause. He had invested in other leaders.

We have great examples from Scripture of men who invested in others to help in the work or to carry it on after they were gone. Moses helped Joshua learn to lead and his investment paid off: Joshua led the children of Israel into the Promised Land. Elijah mentored Elisha and the younger prophet received a double portion of his teacher's spirit. Paul discipled Timothy and Titus and Silas and many more, giving these men affirmation for what he saw in them and opportunity to use their gifts for God's kingdom. Of course, the greatest example in history of investing in leaders is Jesus. Mark wrote,

> "And he appointed twelve (whom he also named apostles) so that they might be with him and he might send them out to preach." (Mark 3:14)

I love that verse. Jesus selected men to be with Him. He spent lots of time with these twelve, and even more with the inner circle, Peter, James and John. He taught them how to preach and pray and lead and love...by His example.

Classic discipleship can be this simple:

1. I do it.
2. I do it and they (the ones I am training) are with me.
3. They do it and I am with them.
4. They do it.
5. They do it and others (the ones they are now training) are with them.

Here's a practical example from my family. I haven't mowed my yard since 1993. That's because my oldest son, Micah, was 9 years old that year and old enough to mow. He had watched me do it many times. I watched him do it several times. Then I let him have it. A few years later, I looked out the window with tears in my eyes to see Micah teaching his younger brother Caleb how to mow. Then Caleb taught Luke, Luke taught Jesse, and Jesse taught Judah. Judah is 18 now, so my years of relative ease when it comes to mowing the yard are about to end. Or, maybe the grandsons can come do it....!

In the church, we ask the men to take turns teaching in home groups every Wednesday night. There is nothing like having to prepare a teaching to help someone really dig into and learn a passage of Scripture. We also ask different men to speak at our monthly men's breakfast. I have a group of nine men who take turns in the worship service on Sundays welcoming the people after the music, going over the memory verse for that week (taken usually from the text I will be preaching), reading the passage we are studying that morning, and praying for me or whoever is preaching. There are also twelve men in the church who have preached for me, and at least four of them have preached in one of our nearby church plants. They are all learning by doing.

I could not agree more with Jeff about playing to your strengths and letting others do the same. The church thrives when all of the people know their spiritual gifts and are actively using them to minister to the body of Christ. There are many people in the church who are much better than I in administration, showing mercy, visiting the sick, counseling, leading worship, handling the finances, repairing the church building, keeping the grounds mowed and cleaned, taking care of infants in the nursery, teaching the young women how to love their husbands (I don't even qualify for that one), and the list goes on and on. It's like a softball team. Every person has to play his position, the one he is most suited for, if the team is going to succeed. The guy playing right field who thinks he should be pitching can be a huge liability for two reasons. He is probably not paying attention to the batter and doesn't see the ball in time as it flies over his head, allowing all three base runners to score. And, he is possibly a thorn in the pitcher's side with his constant "encouragement' that consists of screams that include, "Get the ball over the PLATE, Harry!" Or, "Good grief, just throw STRIKES!" Or, "Don't be afraid to ask the coach for a REPLACEMENT, Harry!" You get the idea.

Daily Tasks

One final thought on working your list for the day. I heard someone say years ago to do the hardest thing on your list first every morning. What a wonderful piece of advice. If I have a hard phone call to make, I want to make it early (after I am prayed up, of course). If I have a hard text to study, I want to tackle it first. Anything I leave until the end of the day, when my energy is depleted and nerves a little frayed, gets done either poorly or not at all.

Reflection Points:

1. Do I like to read? Will I begin to read far and wide to broaden my scope of understanding?

2. Am I loner? Is my wife or family struggling due to lack of relationships?

3. Will I reach out to other pastors to help them or receive from them?

4. Do I waste my time every day or am I focusing on what really matters?

5. Do I feel like I have to control everything or do everything?

Reflection Points: Those Who Support Them:

1. Have I prayed for my pastor that he would keep true to their vision?

2. Do I pray for the pastor and his family to have strong personal relationships?

3. Is there some way I can assist my pastor with his schedule or his usage of technology?

4. Is some gift or talent in my life that I could offer to the pastor for his usage?

Conclusion - Keep on Walking the Witnesses are Cheering!

We are surrounded by a great cloud of witnesses. I wonder what they are saying?

Jeff

In Hebrews 12:1, we encounter this passage:

> *Therefore, since we are surrounded by so great a cloud of witnesses, let us also lay aside every weight and sin which clings to closely, and let us run with endurance the race that is set before us.*

Depending on your personality, you may look at this verse from a couple of different angles. Those who have a bent towards being critical will view these witnesses as a group of people that are watching us to point out where our failure is. The heavenly folks are leaning over the guardrail and examining us to make sure we do not mess up this race. Expecting to hear from these witnesses above something like, "Come on you, straighten up. Do not swerve off the straight and narrow. I ran the race and did well and you better do the same." With this mindset, it would be difficult to find encouragement in this verse.

Some others may lean more toward the witnesses offering encouragement. "Come on, you can make it. I know it's hard. It was hard when we ran that course, but the end is just ahead. Don't quit, don't give in, don't give up. You are almost home; you can do it with God's grace and power."

Which way do you read the verse? Are those who have finished the course offering encouragement or rebukes? Is the emphasis on not messing up, or on finishing strong in spite of failing? I prefer the latter view. As I grow older, I have grown in grace and compassion. The view from over fifty-eight is different from when I was twenty-five. Life has a way of tenderizing us.

I remember watching my mother beat the tar out of a piece of meat with a medieval tool. This event provides a picture for my life. The poor piece of meat lay on a hard surface and then my mother would repeatedly pound it with a heavy metal pointed hammer thing. It seemed so unfair to my mind. My mother simply said that she was tenderizing it.

Life's experiences can be like that. Real pain involving real people hurts really badly. There have been times when I felt like that piece of meat and God was hammering me over and over and over. Blow after blow fell. Not physical, but emotional ones. Trial after trial. Heartache after heartache. I wondered if God was bored and He needed someone to beat up. What time revealed was that He was graciously tenderizing me. Every time I absorbed a blow, something good was finding a home in me. Each strike of the Master's hand gave more insight, compassion, and sensitivity. God is like that. He loves us so much He will inflict pain to bring us to the place of growth and maturity He desires.

Are the witnesses yelling at us to straighten up or to not give up? I don't really know of course, but since they have finished their race, they know what is ahead. If you have read chapter eleven of Hebrews before chapter twelve, you encountered many heroes of the faith. Most of those people spent time on God's table being tenderized. Most of these great men and women of faith failed. Many were disciplined by their loving Heavenly Father. I bet they are shouting out compassion and empathy to us, not railing down on us warnings and rebukes. Those who made it into the hall of faith received grace and after we taste God's grace, we tend to give it a bit more freely.

Rather than chiding us, I believe the witnesses are for us. I have a picture in my mind of walking between two buildings down a long, narrow path. Leaning out of the windows are those that have gone before us down this highway of holiness. Over on the right is Daniel. See him there, three floors up. David is on the left and so is Solomon. There is Gideon and Moses further ahead. I think I see Samson, wow, look at that hair!

What are they shouting? "Come on Jeff, you can make it! Hey, I know the road seems hard sometimes, but God is with you. I know you tripped and fell, but get up and keep on going. Dust yourself off and keep on walking. We are for you. If we made it, you can too. Don't quit, don't give in, and don't give up. The finish line is just there beyond your view, but we can see. You are almost there..."

What about you my reader? Ready to give up? Close to quitting the race? Don't. The finish line is just over the next bend or around the corner. You are so close, and the victory celebration is gearing up for you. Come on, you can make it in Him. If God is for us, who or what can take us out and ruin us? God is for us. I believe the witnesses are cheering for us to finish well. Let's run the race with endurance for we are very close to the end.

Perhaps another illustration will help encourage you. Most of us like a good novel or mystery movie. Suspense builds as we await the conclusion. Page after page of tension and struggle helps add to the joy when the end is revealed. What a boring book or movie it would be if the main character never struggled, failed, or seemed to face impossible odds to overcome.

In our book of life, maybe we are on page thirty or ninety, on our way to two hundred. We are in the midst of a struggle, pressure, heartache and we simply cannot see the way out. We know how our life ends if we are a child of the King. We have the last Book of the Bible and we know we win. As the days and years unfold in our journey, regardless of how bleak they may look, we already know the end. We will be with Jesus. We will look like Jesus. We will rule and reign with the King of Kings and Lord of Lords.

Yes, there is tension, suspense, disappointment, trials, heartache, and difficulties in our story. There has to be if we want to have an exciting ending. There has to be trouble and sorrow in order to reach the glorious conclusion. We can endure because we know the end of our story. We can't quit on page seventy, we have to finish the book to reach the conclusion. Don't quit and keep on walking!

If you are a pastor, you are blessed to serve in a unique way in the Kingdom of our Lord and Savior Jesus Christ. Yes, there are challenges and the battles are real. In the previous pages, we revealed some of them. There are others not covered, but we believe the veil dropped enough to give you a glimpse. You are not alone and others share your battles.

If you are walking in the role of a support to the pastor, we pray you will have a renewed zeal in your efforts. Your pastor needs your prayers and support. May you not grow weary in well doing. Please don't quit. The Kingdom needs you!

Mark

It was the afternoon before my first marathon and my family and I were at the Expo, picking up our packets and looking at all that the vendors had to sell. Our favorite place was a rack of bumper stickers. One said, "If you find me on the road, please drag me across the finish line." Another said, "In my heart I'm a Kenyan." Or, "If you can read this, I'm not in last place!" Or, "This IS my race pace." The next morning, I saw people holding some of the same signs, and many others. Some were signs of encouragement, or, discouragement for the 6,000 runners who passed by. Some people were just trying to be funny, and they were. Like the guy just a half a mile into the race whose sign read, "One. Lousy. Parade." Then there was the lady holding up a sign about ten miles in that said, "My husband knows a shortcut." Or the one that said, "The Kenyans finished an hour ago." Some were meant to be funny, but just were not. When I was in the most pain of the whole experience, at around mile 24, I passed a guy whose sign read, "Is that all you got?" The most encouraging sign I read said, "I am exactly .3 miles from the finish line." That was a sight for sore legs. The only sign that was better than that was the one that actually said, "Finish line."

I thought about that as I preached through 1 Timothy a few years ago. Now, almost at the finish line, Paul held up a sign that is nothing like the one I got at mile 24. Paul doesn't say, "Is that all you got, Timothy?" No. He tells Timothy who he is in no uncertain terms. Paul holds up a sign that says,

"But as for you, O man of God..." (1 Timothy 6:11) Man of God! "Timothy, remember who you are! You are a man of God." I wish we could know somehow what affect that had on Timothy. Did he break into a huge grin when he read that? Or did he break down and weep with relief and thanksgiving?

I know one thing. Paul was inspired by the Holy Spirit to write those words, as he was every word he wrote. The Spirit of God wanted to remind Timothy who he was. A man of God.

He wants you and me to know that, as well.

Reflection Points:

1. What is my view of God the Father? Is He loving, kind and supportive, or harsh, cruel and waiting for me to mess up?

2. If I was walking down the street and the heavenly host was looking at me out of windows what would they say to me?

3. Am I ready to quit? Should I?

4. What would it take for me not to quit or give up? What needs to change for me to finish strong?

Reflection Points: Those Who Support Them:

1. Am I an encouragement to my pastor, or am I a drain?

2. Do I encourage my pastor to keep on walking and not to give up?

3. What could I do or say to help bring encouragement to my pastor?

4. Do I bring joy to my pastor or am I a reason he wants to quit?

Articles:

We wanted to include some thoughts on topics that didn't quit fit into other chapters in the book. We trust as you read these articles that you will prayerfully consider each message and how to live it out for God's glory.

Rethinking Church Staff Positions:
Dr. Jeffrey A. Klick

And he gave the apostles, the prophets, the evangelists, the pastors and teachers, to equip the saints for the work of ministry, for building up the body of Christ (Eph 4:11-12 ESV).

The idea in this verse is that as under-shepherds, we are to be about the business of correcting what is wrong in doctrine, theology, thought patterns encompassing orthodoxy and orthopraxy, and to strengthen and encourage what is healing and redemptive.

Most of us would probably agree that the family unit is broken, or at least in need of strengthening/repair. Divorce statistics for the church at large are close to same as the people that are not born again. Young people are leaving the church in droves. Churches are closing every day and few would argue that we do not have a major problem on our hands in the Church.

I have not performed the research, but based on the last 30 years of experience I would venture to say that the bulk of my counseling time has been devoted to the breakdown of the marriage (communication, $ and sexual issues) and parent/child relational issues.

I have performed detailed doctoral research on what the Bible contains regarding the roles of parents and the organized religious intuitions regarding faith impartation to the next generation. The results were staggering. There are few direct commands to the church either in the New, or in the sanctuary/temple patterns of the Old, regarding the organized religious community's role. There are hundreds directed towards the parent's role and responsibilities, in addition to a great deal of Scripture addressing the marriage relationship.

Perhaps God intended that the parents take the leadership role in such things and that the leaders of the organized community come alongside them to supplement. The traditional family unit is broken and in need of significant repair. What are we who are charged with leading God's people doing about it? If we are serious about reversing the destruction of the family unit, perhaps some new ministry departments or staff positions should be considered as well:

- Staff in charge of strengthening the father in his leadership role in the home
- Pastor in charge of training husbands to love their wives as Christ loved the Church
- Malachi 4:6 curse avoider trainer
- Encouraging the wives and mothers in their Biblical mandate counselor
- How not to destroy your home by your words consultant
- How to be more Christ-like with those that know you best pastor
- Family devotions to implement the pastor's message during the week advisor
- Marriage Stability and Longevity Coordinator
- Divorce prevention pastor
- Reducer of Hypocrisy in the home consultant
- Preparation for being a godly spouse trainer
- Teenage rebellion avoidance ministry leader
- Sibling relationships enhancer
- Helping young people make wise, godly decisions under their parent's authority director

- Giving single adults a purpose in life by serving others leader
- Grandparents as support to parents and not undermine minister

Perhaps you could think of some others. Research indicates that we often spend a great deal of time and money on recovery programs but not all that much on prevention. While parking ambulances at the bottom of the cliff is helpful, stronger guardrails at the top would also seem in order.

The family is the central unit of society and is the plan that God established in His Word for continuity in the faith. Fathers and mothers explaining the truths of God's word to their children is the clear pattern repeated throughout the pages of our Holy Book. God chose a family model out of all the possible ones, being called Father instead of CEO of the universe, or Supreme Executive. He sent His Son, not the VP in charge of Humanity. We are adopted into the family of God; we do not become shareholders of the human corporation. We have many brothers and sisters instead of business partners and again, we are adopted, not merged, absorbed, or taken over. Adam and Eve were the first family, Jesus was born into one, and all of time will end with a marriage feast between Christ and His bride. The traditional family is central to Christianity and its continuance.
If we are to turn the tables on the destruction of the family, we should begin to rethink what our goals are and how to go about implementing change. What specifically am I doing to stem the tide of destruction? Every destroyed family unleashes generational destruction; what will every restored one produce?

A partial answer based on practical observation is that a great deal of effective ministry will come from a functioning home, and very little from a messed up one. As marriages are healed, and relationships restored within the home, outreach to others is a very natural result. Parents reaching their children for Christ are a wonderful fulfillment of the last verse of our Old Testament. This also helps fulfill the great commission. Training our people to reach the potential disciples right under their roof will give good practice as they go out into the highways and byways. Leadership skills learned in the home do transfer to the organized church and world around us. Strong leaders at home can become strong leaders in the Church.

I could go on to qualifications for elders/deacons being tied to the family. How marriage is a picture of the mystery of Christ and the Church. How prayers are hindered by husband/wife relational problems. How power is released when two agree together. How Biblically we cannot delegate away our parenting responsibilities. The stewardship responsibilities tied to our families given by God, etc. but time restraints affect us all. My prayer is that as those charged with fixing things that are broken, we would begin with the ones closest to us, and that we would capture the harvest that is white within our own fields, before we go to far off ones.

Gray Hair Leadership Lessons:
Dr. Jeffrey A. Klick

After more than thirty years in the ministry, here are some battle-tested truths to consider.

1. People are always going to be angry about something.

An old warhorse of a pastor put his graying arm around me in 1981 and said, "Son, just do what is right. People are always going to be mad about something, so just do what is right so when they get mad at you they will be mad for the right reasons." Sage advice that has been proven true over the decades. We cannot please everyone and the goal should be to please the Lord. If the Lord is not happy with our work, then it really does not matter who else is angry. Some people will always be angry; just always do what is right, and then rest because you cannot defend your own reputation. The old saying is true: "Your friends don't need an explanation and your enemies won't believe it anyway."

2. People come and people go.

When I started my own church over twenty years ago, I had an illusion. I honestly believed that everyone would stay forever. Many years ago, I heard from someone, or perhaps even thought this one up myself, I can't remember any longer - "In order to be disillusioned, one first must have an illusion." I had a major illusion that was defeated within the first year of our church plant. Over the years, hundreds of people have come and gone and just about every one of them hurt me in some way or another. It is personal and we must learn how to deal with it personally or it will destroy us.
I have come to the conclusion that some people will remain and become pillars in our church, some are there for a season, and some will never plug in, nor should they. God knows His sheep and where they should be pastured. Our job

is to love, serve, and hold loosely to them, because they are not our sheep, we are undershepherds serving the Great Shepherd.

3. We are in a spiritual battle.

The devil hates you and has a horrible plan for your life, your family, your ministry, and everything else. If we forget that we are soldiers in the Lord's army, we will forget that we have an ancient foe and we will not survive long term. Many leaders have fallen through sexual failure, financial fraud, pride, depression, and a host of other wounds. In the 1970's I had a friend that sang a silly little song that included the phrase, "It's a battlefield brother not a picnic area" or something like that. The picture of bombs blasting around oblivious people sitting around a checkered tablecloth still lingers in my mind. Yes, I know Jesus defeated Satan, but why did Paul bother to write about deception, armor, and those who were faith casualties if there were not still dangers? Why does Jesus rebuke so many of the seven churches in Revelation for chumming up with evil? We are not to be ignorant of our enemy's schemes or we too will join the list of the fallen.

4. We should invest in people.

The Kingdom of God is made up of people, not programs. People are the end, not the means to it. Using people is not godly and not what we are called to do. We are called to equip people, invest in people and release people into service for the Kingdom of Jesus. Every child of God is important and should be viewed as a precious lamb, not simply counted, categorized, and used to expand our egos or bragging rights. People matter as individuals first and groups second.

5. Jesus will do what He said He would do.

Jesus said He would build His Church, and He cannot, nor will not lie. We are part of that plan, but He is the One that will ultimately be successful. One verse that has set me free is

> *O Lord, my heart is not lifted up; my eyes are not raised too high; I do not occupy myself with things too great and too marvelous for me. (Psalm 133:1 ESV)*

Each of us has an area of influence, jurisdiction, and specific calling and none of us is responsible for everything in the Kingdom. That role is reserved for Jesus and He can and will take care of it. Through mass media and instant access to almost everything, we can become discouraged with all the failures, faults, and problems we see in the Kingdom. The truth is there is little we can do about most of it. My frustration, worry, or fear has never changed any of the problems that I observe. My prayers and moving my trust onto the One Who can have done far more at least for my heart and mind.

Jesus will not fail and He does not make junk. He began a good work, He will complete it. Our job is to be faithful in whatever realm He has entrusted to us, and leave the bigger picture to the Master Architect.

These five truths are not the only lessons, but they are foundational in my life and I trust they will assist others who consider them.

Fireproof or Fire Hazard?

Dr. Jeffrey A. Klick

A group of leaders walked into the bank to sign the final papers for their new building loan. Finally, after years of fundraising, the down payment had been raised. As the loan officer pushed the document across the table towards the president of the counsel, soft sobs could be heard from the back of the group. A shaky voice said, "Don't sign it." Everyone turned and stared at the source of the voice, the church treasurer. "Why on earth would you say such a thing?" he was asked. His reply, "There isn't any money, I spent it all. I have a girlfriend..."[17]

Pastors being led away in handcuffs, church staff being fired for stealing and administrators sneaking out of town due to financial mismanagement happen. If fact, it happens more that we might suspect. The news outlets gleefully share the stories. The enemies of Christ rejoice when Christian fraud is exposed, while the church or ministry suffers, and many times slowly dies.

Shocking? Over dramatized? We could only wish it were. Based on research from Miller Management Systems, LLC a Church accounting and management firm based in Kansas City and Springfield Missouri, only about 20% of churches operate in what is known as the "fireproof" condition of ministry. 80% are a "fire hazard" financially speaking.[18]

Fireproof and fire hazard are not referring to the amount of old storage boxes around the furnaces, but to the financial accounting and money management procedures a ministry uses. While we would not be comfortable with attending a

---

[17] Actual case the author worked on while serving as a church administrator.

[18] http://www.mmsmidwest.com/ Research conducted over decades of interaction with hundreds of clients via audits and multiple personal cases handled by Glenn Miller, a Certified Fraud Examiner and president of the firm.

worship service in a facility that was labeled a, "fire hazard," we seem perfectly content to attend the same place where the finances are at risk.

The fact that so many Christian ministries are at risk is indeed bad news. The good news however, is that with some inexpensive changes, most ministries can move from being a fire hazard to nearly fireproof. Does it cost huge amounts of money to make these changes? It costs no more than moving the boxes away from the open flame of the furnace. There might be some inconvenience and a small amount of resistance to implementing change, but isn't it worth it to limit the risk?

Let's look at some of the procedures[19] that can be implemented that will help move any ministry from the danger zone to the safe one. Whenever fraud takes place, it is at least partially due to opportunities being present. Logic would dictate that if we could limit the opportunity, we would limit the instances of fraud. While many of these are or should be obvious, most groups are not implementing them, so they bear repeating.

Cash Receipts

Every ministry receives money. Who handles it, who counts it, how it is deposited and reported will help determine how safe the ministry is. Here are some guidelines that cost nothing to implement.

- Money should always be counted by at least two people. Three is better.
- Checks received in the mail should be opened in the presence of two people.
- Both counters should sign off on the final count sheet.

[19] These procedures are taken from the Fireproofing Your Ministry Workshop conducted by The Institute for Church Management

- Cash should be counted by both counters independently.
- Money counters should rotate to limit the possibility of collusion.
- Counters should not be related.
- All checks should be immediately endorsed with a deposit stamp.
- A duplicate deposit slip should be made out at the time of counting, one copy is deposited, and the other is given to the bookkeeper/accountant.
- These two deposit slips should never be together until after the deposit is made, thus limiting the opportunity for changing the original deposit.
- The bookkeeper/accountant matches the deposit slip processed by the bank, to the contribution database and the General Ledger each month.[20]
- Written instructions are provided explaining exactly what is expected.

If any ministry does all of those steps above, opportunities for fraud will be limited. The actual out-of-pocket expense for the ministry so far is zero.

Cash Disbursements

If a ministry receives any donations, they will eventually spend them. A great deal of fraud takes place during this process, but can be prevented with good controls.

- Every check, with no exception, requires supporting documentation, and two signatures. A signature stamp does not count and will not limit fraud.
- Check signers are not related and not in a direct supervisor/subordinate relationship if at all possible.

---

[20] This is one of the easiest ways to catch fraud yet rarely used. The alteration of a contribution record can be hidden unless this procedure is in place.

- Blank checks are never signed. Ever.
- The same person who generates the check does not sign the check. At least one of the check signers signs all the checks to look for reoccurring patterns.
- Employee reimbursements are made only *after* receiving proper documentation. Petty cash funds should be avoided.
- If credit cards are used, documentation is required for every purchase and is examined by someone other than the user of the credit card. Debit cards should be avoided.
- Voided checks are clearly marked "void," and the signature section is cut off. They are stored in a secure location, never thrown out.
- Bank statements are reviewed by someone other than the one who writes or signs the checks. Even better is to have the bank statement mailed to someone else's location outside of the organization for review.

If any ministry will follows these steps for spending within the organization, the opportunities for fraud will be severely limited. The actual out-of-pocket expense for the ministry so far, remains at zero.

Payroll

Since most ministries will hire employees, it is essential that they follow wise and legal procedures. As recent headlines have shown, the IRS is not overly friendly towards Christian groups, so great care is needed.

- All compensation changes need to be approved by someone other than the employee, and must include appropriate documentation.
- All compensation must be processed through the approved payroll system, including love offerings, special gifts, and bonuses.

- A current W-4 and I-9 is on file for every employee.
- The correct usage of W-2 vs. 1099's is critical.
- Housing allowances, for those that qualify, are approved by the appropriate people before the current year begins.
- All applicable wage and hour guidelines, employee classification, and overtime laws are followed.
- All payroll taxes, and the required reports, are filed in a timely fashion according to the current laws.

The IRS does not play nice and many ministries have been audited and fined for failure to follow the above procedures. While there may be a cost to the ministry to begin to obey the law, this cost is minimal compared to the fines and bad press received if the ministry fails to do so.

Bank/Investment Accounts and Financial Statements

Unless the ministry keeps its funds strictly in cash, financial institutions will be involved. Each of these banks and investment firms issue statements to their customers. The following procedures will provide an additional layer of protection to the ministry.

- A minimum number of bank accounts are used and are balanced to the penny monthly.
- These balances must tie into the General Ledger and the contribution statements.
- Someone other than the person creating the checks should review and balance the statements.
- Strict generally accepted accounting procedures should be used to reconcile and report to the appropriate committees responsible for the funds.
- Financial statements should be timely and complete, and again follow generally acceptable accounting procedures.

All of the above procedures have an extremely low cost to the ministry. Compared to the expense and devastation caused by fraud, the cost is non-existent. Any ministry can implement these guidelines and should. We as Christians should hold to the highest standards in our handling of money and never settle for anything less.

In addition to the above steps, there are a few other issues to be considered in our desire to move to being a fireproof ministry in our finances:

- The consideration of an annual audit from an accounting firm that specializes in Christian ministries. Prices vary depending on frequency and the exact type of review wanted.[21] For example: A simple Compilation typically will range around a few thousand dollars depending on the size of the company. A Review will double that with a full Audit being four times more expensive. Shopping for the best price is mandatory, and make sure you understand your goals and reasons for the services hired.
- If at all possible, try to have a wise, experienced, competent financial officer or treasurer on your board. Someone that understands accounting is very helpful.
- Evaluating and understanding risk and the wise use of insurance[22] is also needed.
- Consider hiring an outside firm to assist with accounting, payroll, and human resources to assure

[21] http://www.kellerowens.com/ An excellent CPA firms that specializes in churches and non-profits

[22] Church Mutual and Guide One Insurance companies are preferred to typical insurance companies. The groups that specialize in churches will understand the unique insurance required.

accuracy, add a measure of separation of duties and a buffer from lawsuits.

Even with all of the above, we can never eliminate every chance of theft or fraud, but we can certainly take these steps to help limit the opportunities and temptations. We can leave our front door open when we go on vacation and just hope all is well, or we can install a deadbolt. We can remove the paint cans and boxes from the open flame by our furnace, or just pray they do not explode. As in so many other arenas of our life, the choice is ours. Choose wisely.

Why Not Lead in Integrity?

Dr. Jeffrey A. Klick

It is interesting that God called His people, better stated, commanded His people, to be holy. Holy is a word that can be defined as "different" or "set apart." In both the Old and New Testament, the command is clear.

> For I am the LORD your God. Consecrate yourselves therefore, and be holy, for I am holy. [23]
> (Leviticus 11:44)

> But as He who called you is holy, you also be holy in all your conduct, (1 Peter 1:15)

If a man on the street poll was taken, I doubt holiness would be the top response to this question:

> **When you think of a Christian leader, what is the first word that comes into your mind?**

While discouraging, it is even more so when we consider the public black eye received when a church leader steals or commits some other form of fraud. The news outlets seem to love freely sharing the sins of the Christian. When a well-known Christian is exposed as a cheat, a thief, immoral or unfair in their dealings, the news receives above the fold exposure.[24]

The Institute of Church Management[25] was created by a good friend of mine. Glenn Miller saw a need for the Church

---

[23] All verses are from the ESV - English Standard Version

[24] In our city anyway, church leadership failures receives front page, full color stories.

[25] The Institute of Church Management is operated by Miller

and Christian ministry arena to step up in its financial integrity. Glenn often asks those attending the workshops offered by the Institute the following question:

> **"Is there any reason why the Church cannot, or should not be, the financial integrity leaders in our communities?"[26]**

The truth is that we all are an example to those around us. Will our behavior be a benchmark or an excuse? When we fail to lead in financial integrity, we provide an excuse for those that do not know Christ. Every time a Christian leader is caught in fraud, the Church suffers shame. Why can't the other side be true? If we would learn to lead with exemplary integrity, our light would shine brighter in the darkness.

The good news is that we can limit the potential damage of fraud through our procedures, and by gaining the appropriate knowledge. The Church does not need to continue down the same old path of failure. There is a movement beginning to change the way the Church does business. At least there should be. If there isn't one yet, then let's you and I begin one today.

The Church of Jesus Christ should be leading the way in financial integrity. Pastors and Christian leaders should be providing answers regarding how to handle money and not gaining headlines through practicing unethical behaviors. We serve the King of Kings. We work as unto the Lord[27], so why shouldn't we be the best in the industry?

Every church or ministry receives and spends money. How we do those two primary activities will reflect our financial integrity. Do we have the proper controls in place to

---

Management Systems, LLC.

[26] Quote taken from "Fireproof Your Ministry" - 2013

[27] Colossians 3:23

discourage fraud? Do we even know what controls are necessary? If not, we are unarmed in a gun battle, and that is always unwise. (Can I still write "gun" in our current political climate?)

The Church is populated with humans. Humans are subject to temptation. Money, and often large quantities of it, is a major temptation to many humans. What are we doing to help those that deal with money to resist or overcome this temptation? How do we know if they are being successful in their struggles? Financial integrity demands that we answer these questions. If we fail to do so, we may find our ministries on the front page of the newspaper, or the subject of thousands of tweets. We may lose them entirely.

Do not despair, there is good news! Churches and Christian ministries can implement policies and procedures that will keep honest people honest. These practices do not have to cost much. In fact, most of them cost nothing at all. Okay, there is the cost of time, and perhaps overcoming the resistance to changing improper behaviors, but these are not financial in nature.

Where do we begin to change? First, there must be a desire to *want to* change. Will you embrace Glenn's challenge to become the leader in financial integrity in your community? Even if no one ever asks you a question about how you handle your finances, you can and should excel. We serve the King of the Universe and anything less than our best is too little and unacceptable.

Second, will you pursue education to learn how to become an excellent leader in financial integrity? No one knows everything, so we all need help. Glenn is a Certified Fraud Examiner.[28]That fact that we have to have such people in the Christian world is disheartening, but leaving that aside for a

---

[28] http://www.acfe.com/

moment, he, and those like him, have a lot of wisdom to share.

In the interest of full disclosure, I help teach along with Glenn at The Institute of Church Management. I have been in full time, paid ministry for over thirty years. For eleven of those years I was the administrator of a large church in my city, and for about the last twenty years, I have served as a senior pastor of my own church. I am therefore somewhat familiar with the inner workings of the church.

While serving as an administrator, I studied and passed the CFP[29] (Certified Financial Planner) professional designation exam. Since becoming a senior pastor, I have completed my Masters degree, a Doctorate and a Ph.D. I know a little bit about studying and learning as well. When I challenge people to keep on learning I am speaking from a position of experience. We must study and we must grow, learn, and adapt.

So, back to my second point; will you pursue the education necessary to learn what needs to be accomplished to protect your ministry? If you don't, who will? If you will not become the leader in integrity in your ministry, who will?

There are tools available to assist you in your pursuit of excellence in integrity. The Institute of Church Management has plenty of them. The National Association of Church Business Administrators[30], and The Evangelical Council for Financial Accountability[31] do as well.

Regarding financial accountability and integrity, Jesus' words still remains true - ask and you will receive, seek and you will find. [32] Lead with integrity and you soon will be

---

[29] http://www.cfp.net/
[30] http://www.nacba.net/Pages/Home.aspx
[31] http://www.ecfa.org/
[32] Matthew 7:7

followed. I know the last words are not Jesus', but they are true nonetheless.

I will leave you with two questions of my own - Will we lead in integrity? If not, why not?

Why Not be Reconciled Today?

J. Mark Fox

Picture three grown sons standing around their father's bed on Christmas, 2005. The four men of the family were together for the first time in at least 15 years. The oldest grew up like many firstborns, wanting to please his dad, working for the company that gave his father a career, being a responsible son. The second son ran off to college, met his wife, and settled 75 miles away from his hometown. His relationship with his father had been strained over the years, sometimes because of his stubbornness and pride, sometimes because of his father's. The third son ran off to the beach after some run-ins with the law, and there he had stayed, without a driver's license but with a job, a moped, and a faithful dog. He too had a strained relationship with his father whose feelings about his third son's lifestyle seemed to alternate between guilt and frustration.

Here they were, all together again, brought to this place because their father was dying. He had been diagnosed three months earlier with cancer, and was doing all that he could to beat the disease. But the prognosis wasn't good, and the weight of their father's impending death muted the sons' laughter and rough teasing. They didn't know what to say. They listened to their father speak about growing up as one of eight children in a house where there were no extras and often not enough love to go around. "The only thing my parents ever gave me," he said, "was a .22 rifle." He went over the finances with his three sons, and began to cry as he spoke of leaving his wife, and their mother, behind.

He said that he had not done a good job when the three boys were growing up of expressing how proud he was of them. "I couldn't have asked for three finer sons," he said. "I just wish I had done a better job giving encouragement and guidance for you three, but when I was growing up, all I got from my dad was the belt...and I guess I passed some of that on." The middle son responded, "Dad, we deserved every lickin' we got...and plenty we didn't get!" The father smiled tiredly and praised his two older sons for the way they had raised their own children. The talk shifted to final plans that would need to be made. "What would you like your obituary to say, Dad?" they asked, and the oldest took notes. "What hymn or scripture would you like in your funeral service?" the middle son asked. His father replied, "How Great Thou Art."

He died a little more than 3 months later. And as the middle son, though I have many regrets about my relationship with Dad, for this one thing I will always be grateful: that the last Christmas we were together, speaking to one another with love, putting the past hurts behind us, loving one another just as Christ has loved us.

I am certain that this is being read by many who are estranged from a brother, a father, a mother. Some have made a vow to themselves that you will "never step foot in *that house again*!" because of past hurts or offenses. Consider this truth: "Bitterness is like drinking poison and waiting for the other person to die." Time is short, friend. Why not be reconciled today, before the sun goes down?

Is it hard? Yes. Is it worth it? Oh, yes.

> "For if you forgive others their trespasses, your heavenly Father will also forgive you..."

The Church Succeeds by Keeping the Main Thing the Main Thing

J. Mark Fox

Perhaps you have heard the old story of the pastor who was asked by a friend visiting from out of town, "How is your church doing?" The pastor said, "Oh, poorly. Very poorly. But, praise the Lord, none of the other churches in the area are doing any better than we are!" It is sad but true that there is often a competitive spirit among churches. Sometimes even marketing strategies are employed in an attempt to lure members away from one fellowship and into another. Part of that can be explained as old-fashioned, selfish greed.

If the culture buys the lie that says, "He who dies with the most toys wins," then the church can buy into it as well. I was in Ghana last summer and had the opportunity to tour a church facility that, when completed, will seat more than five thousand people. I believe the heart of the leadership there is to serve the Lord and minister the Gospel to the people of Kumasi. But there is a danger there that in the midst of building a huge enterprise, they will lose sight of what the church is really supposed to be. A huge church can fail just like a small church can fail: by losing its vision and sense of purpose. A tiny church can be a booming success by keeping the main thing the main thing: God and His glory.

Oh, dear people, you must remember this: the church is not a business venture. It has purposes that go way beyond widgets and sales charts and daily averages. The church is not a college. It boasts of results that the greatest college president in the world cannot even dream of attaining. The church is not here today and gone tomorrow, like Bear Stearns or Circuit City. The church is not in danger of losing its relevance to the culture, like those who built gramophones or who designed eight-track tape technology. Despite the Richard Dawkins' delusions and those of other modern atheists, the church is here to stay because its builder is from everlasting to everlasting.

Not only that, but here is an amazing truth from Scripture: the church is the body of Christ, "the fullness of Him who fills all in all." No business, no college, no political party, no institution of any kind can make that claim. Christ is the head of the church. And the church displays the fullness of Christ to the earth. We cheapen the purpose and the calling of the church when we market it. We bring dishonor to the name of Christ when we compete with one another or when we run the latest gimmick to try to fill the church. God fills it. I don't know about you, but I am not interested in trying to do something only God can do. In the first place, it is foolish because I simply cannot build the church. In the second place, it is deadly for anyone to think that he can and to say something like, "Excuse me, Lord, but I need to help you with your church. Step aside and watch this, God."

How is the church doing? It seems like we are losing the battle. It looks like we need to resort to gimmicks and marketing in order to draw a crowd. It appears that the church is irrelevant and needs to give in and give up. That's only because we are looking around or looking down. Look up! Look at the head of the church, Jesus Christ, and be encouraged. He has already won.

Resources

www.christiandiscipleshipministries.com - Discipleship on steroids
www.hofcc.org - Great network of family churches
www.antiochchurch.cc - Mark's wonderful church!
www.hopefamilyfellowship.org - Jeff's wonderful church!
www.c4fic.org - Resources for the family-oriented church pastor
www.familyintegratedchurch.com - A directory of family-integrated churches
www.foundationrestoration.org - Resources for marriages
www.michael-duncan.net - Friend, co-laborer, excellent author and wordsmith.
www.ambassadorsforchristradio.com - Friends in Panama and radio show hosts.
www.morethancake.org - Friend, teacher, one creative dude.
www.mmsmidwest.com - Accounting, consulting, Institute of Church Management

Bible Study Helps - Free:

www.biblestudytools.com
www.biblegateway.com
www.blueletterbible.org
www.studylight.org/
https://net.bible.org
www.e-sword.net
www.ccel.org

Social Media/Support Ministries - Pastors

www.linkedin.com - There are many pastor forums here
www.plus.google.com/communities - Many pastor groups available
http://www.barnabasministriesinc.org
http://www.pastoralcareinc.com
http://www.shepherd-care.org/index.html

About the Authors:

Jeffrey A. Klick

Dr. Jeff Klick has been in fulltime ministry for over thirty years (since 1981). He currently serves as the senior pastor at Hope Family Fellowship in Kansas City, Kansas, a church he planted in 1993. Dr. Klick married his high school sweetheart, Leslie, in May of 1975. They have three adult children (Andrea, Sarah and David) and ten grandchildren (Lydia, Katelyn, Mackenzie, Daniel, Nathan, Havilah. Addie, Gabe, Alexis, Treya).

Dr. Klick loves to learn and has earned a professional designation: Certified Financial Planner, earned a Master's degree in Pastoral Ministry from Liberty Theological Seminary, a Doctorate in Biblical Studies from Master's International School of Divinity, and a Ph.D. in Pastoral Ministry from Trinity Theological Seminary. In addition to serving as senior pastor at Hope Family Fellowship, Dr. Klick is a consultant with The Institute for Church Management, weekly co-hosts two radio shows, and also serves on the Board of Directors for The Council for Family-Integrated Churches. Dr. Klick is a frequent blogger on several websites and has published multiple books.

Jeff's Books: (Available at Amazon.com)

Courage to Flee: Second Edition - How to achieve moral freedom
Generational Impact: A Vision for the Family - God's plan for the family explained from a Biblical perspective
The Master's Handiwork - God is not finished with any of us yet and He never fails so don't give up or in.
Reaching the Next Generation for Christ: The Biblical Role of the Family and Church - Detailed research on faith impartation to the next generation.

The Discipling Church: Our Great Commission - An in-depth study on the Great Commission
Pastoral Helmsmenship: The Pastor and Church Administration - A handbook and textbook for pastors - a must-have resource for every pastor regardless of church size.

Jeff's Contact Information:

www.jeffklick.com - my personal blog and website

http://www.amazon.com/-/e/B009L3BNLW - My author's page for ordering any of the above books

www.linkedin.com/jeffklick

http://www.facebook.com/jeff.klick.37

https://plus.google.com/115798367168077729314/about

https://twitter.com/jklick

www.hopefamilyfellowship.org - My church

J. Mark Fox

J. Mark Fox is the pastor of Antioch Community Church in Elon, NC, and has taught public speaking at Elon University since 1990. He writes a weekly column for the Times-News of Burlington, NC, which has won five Amy Awards. Mark is the author of six books, Who's Afraid of Public Speaking?, (1998; updated ebook in 2014) Family-Integrated Church (2006), Real Life Moments: A Dad's Devotional. (2008), You Can Write!(2008), Planting a Family-Integrated Church (2008), and his latest, A Faithful Man(2012). Mark and Cindy celebrated 32 years of marriage in June, and have seven children, two daughters-in-law, three grandsons (Blake, Seth, Owen): Micah and Kari, Caleb and Celia, Hannah, Luke, Jesse, Judah and Susanna, ages 29 to 15. Mark's passion is preaching and writing, and he enjoys running and traveling.

Mark's Books: (Available at Amazon.com)

Who's Afraid of Public Speaking?

A Faithful Man: Equipped to Lead as Prophet, Priest, Protector and Provider

Planting a Family-Integrated Church

Family-Integrated Church

Real Life Moments: a Dad's Devotional

Mark's Contact Information:

markfox57@gmail.com

www.jmarkfox.com - my personal blog

www.linkedin.com/pub/j-mark-fox/95/493/aa7

http://www.facebook.com/jmarkfox

www.healthychurchradio.com - my podcast

https://twitter.com/jmarkfox

www.antiochchurch.cc

Thank you for reading our thoughts Keep the faith and finish strong!

For everyone who has been born of God overcomes the world. And this is the victory that has overcome the world—our faith. (1 John 5:4)

Made in the USA
San Bernardino, CA
16 November 2014